# MEREVALE CHURCH AND ABBEY

For Neville and Sheila
With my love and
best wishes — it's
just great to meet up
again after so long
— with happy memories
of the Liverpool days,

John

August 27:
2005.

*The Church of Our Lady, Merevale*

# MEREVALE CHURCH AND ABBEY

THE STAINED GLASS, MONUMENTS AND HISTORY
OF THE CHURCH OF OUR LADY AND
MEREVALE ABBEY, WARWICKSHIRE.

JOHN D. AUSTIN

BREWIN BOOKS

First Published by Brewin Books,
Studley, Warwickshire. B80 7LG, April 1998

*Front cover:* The prophet Isaiah, from the Jesse Window 1330-1340
The Church of Our Lady, from the east

## For  GILL
## with love.

ISBN Hardback  1  85858  115  X

ISBN Paperback  1  85858  114  1

British Library Cataloguing-in-Publication Data
A Catalogue record for this book is available from The British Library

Typeset in Palatino and made and printed in Great Britain
by Warwick Printing Co. Ltd., Warwick CV34 4DR

# CONTENTS

## Notes

Notes are placed at the end of each section with author,
date of publication and page number. Full details are
given in List of References and Bibliography.

# ACKNOWLEDGEMENTS

I would like to put on record my sincere and grateful appreciation of the characteristic generosity of my wife, Gill. Without her help this book would not have been published.

I am also very much indebted to the following people who, over the years, have helped me with this book – Sir William Dugdale, Bt, for access to the Dugdale archives and for writing the Foreword – Sarah Brown of the Royal Commission on Historic Monuments of England for teaching me about stained glass, a great deal of help generally, and writing an Introduction – Edith Hudson and the late Dorothy Hudson, my first encouragers – the Rev. Derek Carrivick and Dennis Chapman, Rector and Churchwarden of Merevale Church – Bro. Jonathan, O.C.S.O., Archivist, of Mount St Bernard Abbey – Prof. Richard Marks, Dr Christopher Norton and the Peter Newton Bequest at the Centre of the Medieval Studies Department of York University – the late George Wilkie who drew the plans of the Abbey – Penelope Winton of the York Glazier's Trust for much help and permission to print the ground plan of the windows – Rita Callwood – David Pykitt – Dr David Park of the Courtauld Institute of Art – Thomas Woodcock, Norroy and Ulster King of Arms, College of Arms – Dr David Walsh of the University of Rochester (New York) and Dr Sue Wright of Reading University, both of the Bordesley Abbey Excavation team – Rafe Clutton of Cluttons, Chartered Surveyors – Dr Ben Benedikz of Birmingham University – Dr Levi Fox of the Dugdale Society – Michael Farr and Christopher Jeens, County Archivists of the County Record Office, Warwick – Dr Alan Barnes – the staff at Atherstone Library – Charles Clarke – Rev. Stan Marriott – Canon Peter Buckler – Robert Hughes – Rev. S. A. Mairs – Peter Stockham for publishing guidance – Amanda Daws for doing the window diagrams – Mabel Walters for listing churchyard names – Bill Powell – Celia Parton for loan of the portrait of W.S.Dugdale – Joyce Field and Loraine Kimberley for secretarial work – and John C. Lock and Dr G. W. Nicholls for proof reading, advice, much help and friendly encouragement.

For copyright permission I am very grateful to the RCHME and to Anna Eavis of the National Monuments Record Centre for colour photographs, to Faber and Faber for the T.S. Eliot quotations, to Martin Harrison for material from his *Victorian Stained Glass*, to Penelope Hunting for quoting from her unpublished biography of Henry Clutton, to Birmingham City Archives for the drawing of Merevale Abbey (from the Aylesford Collection), and the General Editor of the *Victoria County History of Warwickshire* for the plans of Merevale Church and the Abbey Ruins and material from volume lV, on p. 142 (footnote 4), 143 (5), 144 (9), 145 (10 and 11), 146 (13). The prayer on the last page is by the Rev. Dr William Bright (1824-1901).

# LIST OF ILLUSTRATIONS

# FOREWORD

## by Sir William Dugdale, Bt

It is a great pleasure to be asked to contribute a Foreword to this painstaking and devoted account of Merevale Church. John Austin has delved into the past and uncovered a vast amount of information, discovering documents that would otherwise have mouldered away. It will provide a mine of information for people who wish to study the Church of Our Lady at Merevale.

It is interesting to think that, since its consecration, Mass was said every day until the Dissolution in 1538, and services have been conducted since that date without fail on Sundays up to the present day. The Monastery no doubt found that the pressure of pilgrims to touch the miraculous statue of the Virgin interfered too much with their rigorous devotions. As a result they set up the Chapel to alleviate this problem which to this day remains the focus of all parochial activity. Next year will be the 850th anniversary of the foundation of the Abbey so the publication of this book is a very timely enterprise.

Anyone who has an interest in fine stained glass, the medieval monastic life and indeed the history of Warwickshire, should read this book on Merevale Church because it really is a repository of facts and information which cannot be found elsewhere. My congratulations to John Austin for this volume which will add greatly to the knowledge of our parochial history.

August 1997

# PREFACE

'A people without history
Is not redeemed from time, for history is a pattern
Of timeless moments. So while the light fails
On a winter's afternoon, in a secluded chapel
History is now and England.'

Thus wrote T. S. Eliot with Little Gidding in mind. It could, however, easily have been Merevale that inspired him, or one of the other thousand out-of-the-way churches of rural England. Individually they are often architectural gems and contain a small selection of nationally important items. Together they contribute greatly to the wealth of our heritage. This book is about one of them.

The Church of Our Lady, the Gate Chapel of Merevale Abbey, survived the Dissolution and, as Sarah Brown says in her Introduction, is one of the most important repositories of the Cistercian decorative arts in England, containing tiles, woodwork, what may prove to be the earliest surviving Cistercian wall-painting in the country and stained glass that constitutes 'the most substantial and informative of all surviving Cistercian window decoration' [1]. Some of the glass probably came from the great church of the Abbey, for example the Jesse window, and some is in the position for which it was made, the *in situ* glass. It has been said that the Jesse window 'shows a perfection of design hardly to be found elsewhere in England'.[2] These are the corner stones on which work was started.

The core of the book is therefore a full description of the medieval glass, and to this has been added the Victorian windows, and the monuments. However to make it as comprehensive as possible chapters have been added on Stained and Painted Glass, and on the Tree of Jesse and Jesse windows. The book starts with the history of the Abbey, followed by a description of the ruins and the Gate Chapel, and the successive owners from the Dissolution to the present - the Deveraux, Stratford and Dugdale families. There are biographical notes on architects, archaeologists, and stained glass window manufacturers, and details of the rood screen, the wall painting, the floor tiles, the books in the abbey library, and many other subjects. There is also an index of every name in the churchyard. On a slightly different note there are brief insights into two unusual aspects of the religious life of the Church. Monument **M22** gives details of a letter of 1361 from the Bishop of Lichfield and Coventry concerning pilgrims at the time of the Black Death. The letter refers to 'the great multitude of the faithful who almost daily pour to the Chapel built beside the gateway of your monastery', some being 'brought to the point of death by the crush of people.' Appendix D contains three letters of 1687 relating to the problem of the incumbent, who was illegally allowing Nonconformists to preach at Merevale.

Before proceeding further there is a general point which I would like to make. It could be referred to as 'the importance of seeing Merevale in a broad landscape'. It is fascinating to realise that almost everything relating to the Church can, and indeed should, be seen in a wider context. To start with, the Jesse window is stylistically related to other windows of a similar date made probably at the same glazier's workshop. To try to understand one Jesse window it is helpful to know some of the others, at Lowick, Ludlow and Madley. Likewise the ornaments in the design, the winged dragons for instance, can be related to illuminated manuscripts and sculpture of the same period, for example in a Book of Hours in the Walters Art Gallery in Baltimore, and to Romanesque capitals in the Cathedral of Santiago de Compostella in Spain. The birds in the design can be compared with the Bestiary section of Queen Mary's Psalter and birds in the wall painting at Longthorpe Tower in Northamptonshire.[3] Taking the monuments next, it is helpful in understanding the Ferrers's effigy in the nave, to know about similar effigies in The Temple Church in London. The alabaster tomb-chest is more interesting with the knowledge of a similar one, made from alabaster from the same quarry, at Willoughby-in-the-Wolds in Nottinghamshire. Much can be learned about the Victorian windows by seeing other examples by the same manufacturers. The work of Henry Clutton, the Victorian architect who excavated the Abbey, completed Merevale Hall, restored the church and built the Archway, is understood better if his other works are known, including the twelfth-century French Gothic church at Moorhouse in Nottinghamshire. Indeed the church itself with its architectural problems, including the unusually large chancel, is better understood by considering other Cistercian Gate Chapels such as those at Kirkstead, Furness and Tilty. To stand on the site of the Gate Chapel at Bordesley Abbey, near Redditch, the mother house, and to look down over the fields to where the Abbey buildings stood, with the stream which was the monk's water supply on your right, flowing from west to east, is to be at Merevale with a difference. Indeed every Cistercian Abbey is a guide to the others; to know something of one is to know something of them all.

Merevale, therefore, may be a small and forgotten church of rural England, but it can also be seen as a microcosm reflecting much of great interest and value of medieval art and history in the broader national landscape.

In the course of writing about the Church and the Abbey, events sometimes occur which appear unrelated, but in fact have a direct effect on one another. For example in 1332 Edward III granted the Abbey the toll for three years on goods passing over Felden bridge and for its repair. In 1338 the monks were given land at Overton, Peatling and Bruntingthorpe, and in 1343 they were granted a market and fair in Atherstone. In 1345 William de Henore gave land in Atherstone, Bentley and Baxterley to endow a Chantry for his soul and that of his ancestors.[4] This was all extra income but there were also new expenses. In about 1343 there was a fire at the abbey and Pope Clement 1V gave more land to help the repair work. Together with donations to the statue of Our Lady there must have been a general increase in their wealth. Firstly, the entire south aisle was built, possibly to accommodate the Chantry. Secondly, the floor of the nave was re-laid with heraldic 'Nottinghamshire' tiles (a few of which remain). Lastly, the south chancel arch wall painting, originally a masonry pattern design of 1240, was repainted with a large figurative design. Without knowledge of the reasons for the increased income, the improvements, which are all of around 1340-50, would be hard to explain. This is covered in detail in Chapter 1.

With the passing centuries, however, the thread of history at Merevale has sometimes become entangled. One problem is the difficulty in identifying and dating some of the memorials and other items. In particular there are questions relating to the Jesse glass (Window **1**), two monuments (**M18** and **M39**), and the Rood Screen (Appendix E). All these difficulties stem from the fact that the church was the Gate Chapel. Various items were moved to the chapel from the conventual church for safe-keeping at various times. In most churches the date of a fixture is when it was put there. This is not so at Merevale. The detective work used to try and unravel these, and others knots, is explained in the text.

There is also the question of the statue of the Virgin, which was in the church for over three hundred years. It is quite possible that the south aisle was originally built to contain a chapel dedicated to Our Lady, and that the reason for the unusually large chancel was to accommodate pilgrims over the centuries. For the arguments for this theory see The Gate Chapel in Chapter 1.

In his Introduction to *A Bibliography of Stained Glass* David Evans wrote 'Stained glass windows have been the object of scholarly research and popular exposition for some time. However advances in knowledge have not been made systematically, and it is not too much to say that the subject remains at the level of "primitive accumulation".'

It is not too much to say that the whole of this book is the result of 'primitive accumulation'.

John D. Austin

1    Richard Marks in Norton and Parks 1986, p 223.
2    Rackham 1930, p 91.
3    Newton 1961, p 39.
4    Salzman vol.4 1947, p 147.

*The Church of Our Lady, Merevale West Front*

# INTRODUCTION

by

Sarah Brown.

In 1538, when Henry VIII suppressed the monasteries throughout his kingdom, there were over one hundred houses owing allegiance to the Cistercian Order. The first Cistercian house, Waverley (Surrey), was founded in 1128. By the 1150s forty-five monasteries had come under Cistercian control. They were to become one of the most powerful and influential forces in the intellectual, artistic and religious life of the realm. With their close links to the Order's houses in Burgundy, and with their abbots attending the annual Chapter at Citeaux, the English Cistercians became an important conduit for Continental architectural ideas, so much so that they have been called the 'missionaries of Gothic'.[1]   And yet relatively little survives of the Cistercian architectural and artistic heritage. Some of their greatest houses are among the most romantic and most-visited ruins in England – Rievaulx, Fountains, Tintern. Others, transformed into residences for the nobility, are visited by thousands who probably never realise that they are on monastic sites once chosen for their seclusion – Beaulieu and Woburn are now better known for their leisure attractions than for the monks who once lived there.

Most accounts of Cistercian art and architecture have stressed the Order's early prohibition of figural and coloured images inside its churches, enshrined in its legislation and most eloquently voiced by St Bernard's *Apologia* of c.1124-52. The Capitula of c.1122-c.1135 forbade all coloured, figural decoration, except for a painted wooden cross, a stipulation that remained in force into the thirteenth century. The statutes of c.1145-1151 extended the prohibition to stained glass – only white glass, without crosses or pictures, was admitted in a Cistercian church and in 1159 those churches with coloured windows made before the ban were given three years to remove and replace them.[2]   These strictures led to the evolution of a number of types of decoration that have been identified as distinctively Cistercian. White masonry decoration was permitted and a number of geometric and vegetal motifs are common to masonry decoration, uncoloured grisaille window glass and tile pavements.[3] Whether these motifs can be regarded as exclusive to the Cistercian order is debatable. Recent studies of Cistercian grisaille window glass have questioned the exclusivity of this type of glazing and raise the question of whether the Cistercians were originators or merely adapters of a type of glazing used in other monastic, religious or secular contexts.[4] By the end of the thirteenth-century the rules against figural and coloured images were being ignored and stained glass, wall and panel paintings began to be introduced into Cistercian churches whose communities were apparently unable to resist the pressures of wealthy lay patronage. The early fourteenth-century wall paintings in the *capella ante portas* (gatehouse chapel) at Hailes (Gloucestershire) are hardly distinguishable from a high-quality scheme conceived for a parish church and the scenes of hunting and figures of hybrid grotesques have a distinctly secular flavour [5] By the end of the Middle Ages even the Abbots of Cistercian houses were supporting the introduction of the figural and decorative arts into their churches. At Meaux Abbot William of Scarborough (1372-96) had adorned the altars of St Benedict and of St Peter with panels and images, while William Angell, the last abbot of Sawtrey (Hunts) had paid personally for the glazing of a window at the west end of the church.[6]

When the Dissolution came, it was the Cistercians of all the Orders that suffered most severe losses of buildings and their furnishings. The churches of the Benedictines, less remotely located in better-populated areas, might survive as a parish church (Tewkesbury) or as cathedral churches of a newly-created diocese (Gloucester). The founders of Cistercian houses had deliberately sought out remote and secluded locations, and paid the price for their solitude at the Reformation. While Cistercian churches at Abbey Dore and Margam were to survive in parochial use, plans to turn Fountains into the cathedral of a new northern diocese and Rewley into a college came to nothing[7]. Many sites were demolished for their valuable building materials and even royal patronage in the past was no insurance against destruction – of Hailes in Gloucestershire, founded by Richard of Cornwall, brother of Henry III, little but the gatehouse chapel survives above ground.

Whether demolition or adaptation into a secular residence was the fate of a Cistercian monastery, the fate of the furnishings, liturgical vessels, vestments and books used in the conventual church was always the same. Plate, lead, glass and other valuables were inventoried, valued and sold. Stained glass was sometimes salvaged for re-use. At Rievaulx, for example, the stained glass was sorted into three categories and only the third of these was stripped of its lead.[8] The churchwardens of Wing (Bucks) bought a window from nearby Warden Abbey, while the bishop of Worcester's servant bought the glass from the cloister of Bordesley Abbey.[9] None of this glass has survived. Only Abbey Dore has retained medieval glass in the conventual church, and that in a fragmentary and diminished state.[10]

The Cistercian monastery of Merevale, founded in 1148 as a dependent of Bordesley in Worcestershire, was one of the three Cistercian foundations in Warwickshire. Stoneleigh was also part of the Bordesley 'family'[11], while Combe owed allegiance to Waverley. The building history of Merevale has not yet been properly elucidated; excavations in 1849 uncovered the size and shape of the church but the site has never been subjected to thorough professional archaeological analysis. The *capella ante portas* is the only substantial survival from the monastic complex. It survives as one of the most important repositories of the Cistercian decorative arts in England, containing tiles, woodwork, what may prove to be the earliest surviving Cistercian wall-painting in the country and stained glass that constitutes 'the most substantial and informative of all surviving Cistercian window decoration'.[12]

At the surrender of the monastery on 13 October 1538, the inventory included 'the particion of olde tymber in the body [nave] of the curche' (valued at 1s.), 'the glass and iron in the wyndeys of the curche' (2s.) and 'xxviii panys of payntyd glass' in the cloister.[13] In the east window of the present church is part of a large Tree of Jesse of c.1320-40, clearly made for a far larger window than the fifteenth-century tracery that it now fills. While it cannot be proved that the Jesse Tree came from the lost conventual church, such a subject would have been entirely appropriate in the church of a Cistercian house, an Order with a special devotion to the Virgin Mary. It is clear that other items were salvaged and brought to the gatehouse chapel at various times. The screen now at the west end of the church is likely to have originated in the abbey church. The leg of the partial effigy of a thirteenth-century knight, whose torso was found early in the nineteenth-century, was recovered from excavations on the site of the chancel in 1849 (see monument **M18**). The conventual church remains the most likely provenance of the Jesse Tree.

This would make it one of the most extensive stained glass survivals from a Cistercian location. In its present form, shorn of the recumbent figure of Jesse, the image of the Crucified Christ and the Virgin Mary, it fits a five-light window, but must once have filled a far larger one. The single heads of prophets and kings scattered across the perpendicular tracery lights suggest that the original window tracery may have been reticulated; single heads were used in this way in Jesse Tree window at Ludlow (Shropshire) and Madley (Herefordshire). More interestingly, the Merevale Jesse offers further proof that the Cistercians were employing secular craftsmen to decorate their buildings. On stylistic grounds the window can be identified as the product of a workshop that made windows for Worcester Cathedral, for the bishop of Worcester's parish church of Kempsey, for the parish church of Hadzor (Worcestershire) and some figures in the Latin Chapel of the Augustinian priory of St Frideswide in Oxford (now Christ Church Cathedral). The abbey of Merevale was enriched in the late 1320s and early 1330s (see Chapter 1), perhaps a period of some refurbishment of the church at a time when earlier prohibitions of stained glass were being overlooked.

The provenance of the other glass in the church is far less problematic, as it represents *in situ* glazing of some interest, helping to elucidate the building history of the chapel itself. The gatehouse chapel of a Cistercian house was of considerable importance, as it was accessible to pilgrims, visitors and a lay congregation. The stained glass reveals that by the middle of the fourteenth-century the chapel was attracting lay benefactions in a manner very similar to a parish church. Indeed, it is probably because the chapel had come to serve a parochial purpose that it survived complete neglect and destruction at the Reformation. Two donor panels, one depicting two knights of the Ferrers family (now lost) and another depicting Sir John de Hardeshull and his wife (now in the National Gallery in Melbourne) were recorded in the south aisle by Dugdale,[14] and can probably be associated with the redevelopment of the south aisle of the chancel that took place c.1345 when a chantry was founded there. It was in this period that an image of the Virgin Mary in the gatehouse chapel began to attract significant numbers of pilgrims. By 1361, when plague was once again a scourge, the number of pilgrims was so great that arrangements for a special penitentiary had to be made.[15]

That the chapel remained an important site for the veneration of the Virgin Mary is clear from the fact that as late as 1535 the offerings at the image were still worth the significant sum of £2 per annum.[16] Glass on the north side of the church relates to an early sixteenth-century rebuilding of the north chancel chapel. Antiquarian accounts recorded the name of two donors associated with the work. One was Thomas Skevington, a monk of Merevale and bishop of Bangor, who gave a window that recorded the date of his death, 1533. Another window was given by John Handewell, former reeve of Coventry, who was buried in the church c.1524.[17] The main light glazing has almost completely disappeared, but part of the Assumption of the Virgin survives, although the loss of her head suggests deliberate defacement of an image that would have been judged superstitious after the Reformation that was so soon to lead to the abbey's demise.

Sarah Brown
December 1997

1    The concept of the Cistercians as 'missionaries' of a new architectural idiom was first expressed in the 1850s. It has been reassessed and vindicated in a northern English context by Dr Christopher Wilson in 'The Cistercians as missionaries of Gothic in Northern England' in Christopher Norton and David Park (eds) *Cistercian Art And Architecture In The British Isles*, Cambridge 1986, pp 86-116.
2    Christopher Norton, 'Table Of Cistercian Legislation', in Norton and Park 1986, pp 317-393.
3    See contributions on these subjects in Norton and Park 1986.
4    Helen J. Zakin, *French Cistercian Grisaille Glass*, New York and London 1979; for an overview of the English material see Richard Marks, *Stained Glass in England During The Middle Ages*, London 1993, pp 127-133.
5    David Park, 'Cistercian wall painting and panel painting' in Norton and Park 1986, pp 200-204.
6    Peter Fergusson, *The Architecture Of Solitude*, Princeton 1984, p 144; Park in Norton and Park 1986, p 209.
7    Fergusson 1984, p 158.
8    Fergusson 1984, p 158.
9    Richard Marks, 'Cistercian window glass in England and Wales' in Norton and Park 1986, p 211; Fergusson 1984, p 158.
10   Royal Commission on Historical Monuments (England), *An Inventory of Historical Monuments in Herefordshire, I, South-West*, London 1931; Marks in Norton and Park 1986, pp 214 and 219-220.
11   Flaxley in Gloucestershire was the fourth member of the Bordesley 'family'.
12   Richard Marks in Norton and Park 1986, p 223.
13   L.F.Salzman (ed), *Warwickshire*, Victoria County History, vol 11, p 78
14   William Dugdale, *The Antiquities of Warwickshire*, London 1656, p 783.
15   VCH Vol. II, p 76.
16   VCH Vol. II, p 77.
17   Marks in Norton and Park 1986, pp 222-223.

# CHAPTER 1

*History of Merevale Abbey,
a Description of the Abbey Ruins
and the Gate Chapel.*

*History of Merevale Abbey*

In 1098, exactly nine hundred years ago, a group of twenty-one dissenting Cluniac monks, anxious to lead a life closer to the simple beauty of the ideals of St Benedict, left the Burgundian abbey of Molesme. Under Abbot Robert they established a new community at Cîteaux, fourteen miles south of Dijon. Stephen Harding, an Englishman, consolidated the group and in 1119 a petition was made to the Pope to constitute them as a new order. With St Bernard as the third abbot the expansion was electrifying in its popularity. When Merevale was founded in 1148, exactly fifty years later, there were forty-five Cistercian monasteries in England and a total of 399 in Europe. By the year 1200 the number had risen to 525.

Often situated in secluded valleys or other places of required remoteness, where the confines of nature emphasise the man-made walls, the abbeys of the Cistercians rest in a compelling harmony with their surroundings.[1] Merevale Abbey is no exception.

In the turbulent times of King Stephen, who was constantly warring with his cousin, the Empress Matilda, the monastic life must have seemed very attractive. Not only did it appeal to the spiritual aspirations of the prospective monk but also to the founders of the Abbeys. A wealthy nobleman could take out a two-sided insurance. He could pay taxes and lend men to help fight for the King on the one hand, and establish an abbey to keep in with Pope on the other. As a bonus he might save his soul. Similarly Robert, Earl Ferrers was no exception when he founded Merevale in 1148.

For ease of reference and for a taste of his style the description of Merevale from Sir William Dugdale's *Antiquities of Warwickshire,*1656, is given in Appendix G.

Here then, at Merevale, the first wooden structures of the abbey were built, in what Dugdale calls 'this mountainous and woody desert (as fitting for solitude and devotion)'. It was settled by monks from Bordesley Abbey in Worcestershire. By reason of its situation it was named Miravalle – wonderful valley. Ferrers endowed the Abbey with land including 'all his Forest of Arden, i.e. his Out-wood in that part of the Woodland, which then bore the name of Arden',[2] and much more.  This grant, and those of subsequent benefactors, was confirmed by Henry II some time before 1170. The Founder died in 1170 and was buried in the abbey in a salted ox-hide. In 1254 William, fourth Earl Ferrers of Chartley, died and as Patron of the abbey was buried in the Chapter House (see monument **M18**). Edward I stayed at the abbey on 16-17 August and 17 September 1275.

The Register of the Abbey, which was consulted by Sir William Dugdale and the Leicestershire antiquary William Burton in the seventeenth century has been lost. The history has therefore to be compiled from official records and indirect sources.

By 1297 the circumstances of the abbey had became impoverished and Peter de Leicester, at the request of the Chapter, was appointed by the crown as custodian. No sheriffs, bailiffs or other minister of the king were to be accommodated at the abbey without his consent.

Edward II visited the abbey on 10 March 1326 and two days later confirmed the Founder's grants.

In February 1328 Petronill Oliver, of Leicester, gave the abbey two messuages, three shops, and a yearly rent of 12s. in Leicester, to pay for a priest to celebrate the Divine Office daily in the conventual church for her soul and those of  her ancestors.

Whilst staying at the abbey  in March 1332 Edward III granted the monks the toll for three years on goods passing over Felden bridge and for its repair. In 1343 the monks were also granted a market and fair at Atherstone, while Pope Innocent III gave the monks the church of Orton on the Hill and its two chapels. Shortly before 1344 fire damaged the abbey and in response to the petition of Henry of Lancaster, Earl of Derby, Pope Clement VI granted the appropriation of the chapels of Twycross and Gopsall. In 1357 John de Lisle granted to the abbey a messuage and a virgate of land at Bentley, of which he was lord of the manor, to pay for fifteen candles to burn in the Church of Our Lady outside the gate of the abbey.

In spite of the cost of repairing the fire damage the period 1340-1350 also seems to have been a time of growth and development. As will be seen, the Church of Our Lady received a new south aisle for a Chantry and also perhaps to display the statue of Our Lady, new floor tiles, and major additions to the wall painting.

In June 1361, Bishop Stretton, of Lichfield and Coventry, commissioned Brother Thomas de Leycester, a monk of Merevale, to act as penitentiary for the pilgrims who frequented the Gate Chapel. It is stated in the licence that the bishop had been informed that large numbers of pilgrims were coming to the chapel, and by reason of the crush and various prevalent diseases, many were brought to the point of death. Full power was therefore granted to absolve those penitents who were in extremity. It is interesting to note that the *Secunda Pestilencia* of the fourteenth century raged in England during the summer of 1361, particularly in Warwickshire. This appointment was made during the bishop's pleasure, but  it was  renewed to the same monk for penitents at the Gate Chapel ten years later. (see Monument **M22**)

The abbey purchased land in 1386 in Atherstone, Whittington and Baxterley, in Tamworth and Wilnecote, but in spite of these and other accessions to the endowment of the abbey additional assistance was needed, and in 1401 the Pope granted indulgence to all contributing to the repair of the abbey church during the next ten years. In 1450, when John Buggeley was abbot, a licence was obtained to appropriate the church of Mancetter.

Henry V11 visited the abbey in September 1503.

In a list of debtors that Thomas Cromwell drew up in February 1522, is the name of William (Arnold), abbot of Merevale.  A letter of William Brabazon to Cromwell in September of the same year gives a broad hint as to the nature of the debt, which, to put it plainly, was an unpaid promised bribe.  The letter states that the abbot of Merevale is very short of money, but at Christmas he will pay most part of his 'duty' to Cromwell; meanwhile he forwarded 53s.4d. as a reward to Cromwell's trouble about his election.  In January, 1532, he sent the sum of 4 marks to Cromwell for his own use, stating he was 'sore charged that year through barrenness of corn.' In a very long list of bribes received from religious houses in 1536 occurs 'the abbot of Merevale – £4.'

In July 1535 Nicholas Austen, abbot of Rewley in Oxfordshire, wrote to Cromwell, begging his favour for one of his brethren to secure for him the appointment as abbot of Merevale, which he understood to be vacant. A considerable bribe was promised Cromwell if this was done.

There was, however, no vacancy: William Arnold was returned as abbot in the *Valor Ecclesiasticus* report of this year and remained to the end.  The report gave the clear annual value of Merevale as £254. 1s. 8d.  The two churches of Mancetter and Orton on the Hill were valued together  at £73 4s. 8d.  The considerable sum of £50 from their rents were reserved for expenditure on hospitality for wayfarers or other guests.  The offerings at the statue of our Lady averaged £2 a year. Alms which were given to the poor at the gates on Maundy Thursday were 5s., twelve quarters of barley made into loaves, three quarters of barley made into beer, and  3,000 herrings. The total value amounting to £6 3s. 0d. In addition to this there was a weekly dole at the monastery gate of oaten bread and beer, which cost the house £5 13s. 8d. a year.

It is perhaps interesting to compare the Abbey's income with that of the Austin Friars in Atherstone, which was a poor house indeed. In 1535 their income was £2 18s. 0d. out of which they had to pay £1 6s. 8d. to the Abbey as ground-rent. After other expenses they had a clear income of £1 10s. 2d.

On 20 July 1537, Abbot Arnold wrote to Cromwell acknowledging the receipt of the Lord Privy Seal's orders to lease Newhouse Grange to Richard Cromwell, his nephew, for sixty years.  The chapter had no option but to agree, and the abbot wrote that Lord Ferrers, their patron, would shortly bring the sealed lease with him to London.  He added that Cromwell's had earlier stopped Mr Robert Finder's application for their grange, which could not really be spared as they had leased other pastures to many of Mr Richard Cromwell's friends at his request.  They begged his lordship to consider this, a request that the Lord Privy Seal apparently ignored.

On 13 October 1538, the surrender of this house was signed, being made over to Visitor Legh for the king's use.   The signatures are those of William Arnold, the abbot, John Ownsbe, the sub-prior, and eight of the other monks.   The abbot obtained the considerable pension of £40; the sub-prior and four monks each £5. 6s.8d.; three monks £5 each, and one only 3s. 4d.

This account relies heavily on Saltzman.

A full inventory of the contents of the Abbey was taken and is printed in Appendix G.

The late Sir William Dugdale, Bt (1872-1965), wrote that the two Commissioners, responsible for the inventory and sale, said in their report that they had heard that the Abbot had sold £38 worth of silver plate to one Warren, a goldsmith. Afterwards they confessed that the Abbot had given them this money 'in order that they might be good masters to him and his brethren'. The matter was reported to the King and the affair was investigated by the Surveyor General. It appears that nothing happened to the Commissioners who probably passed on the bribe they had received to save their own heads.[3]

In this sad and sordid way four hundred years of monastic life at Merevale came to an end. As the monks were dispersed, their way of life and their buildings disappeared forever. Where recently stood church, cloister, barn and guest house there now lay deserted ruins. Merevale, in one aspect, was immeasurably fortunate in that the Church of Our Lady survived, enabling us today 'to guard, preserve, delight in, brood upon; and in these transitory fragments scan the immortal longings in the soul of man' – Walter de la Mare.

*Description of the Ruins*

Of the great abbey church the only masonry that remains above ground is a twenty-foot section of the south wall of the south aisle. The site was partly excavated in 1849 by Mr William Stratford Dugdale and  Henry Clutton the architect, and apparently only enough was discovered to identify the size and shape of the church.[4] Clutton's report, of 1850, includes the following -

'With the kind permission and assistance of Mr Dugdale, who placed a considerable staff or workmen at our disposal, the excavations were commenced. The area formerly occupied by the conventual church is now unfortunately a rick yard. It is painfully evident that the ruins of this abbey, like many others, have been the stone quarry of the neighbourhood, and worked too with a spirit to wring from them every available stone for building purposes; under such treatment it is only to be wondered at that the few remains which do exist, should have been preserved at all'. They uncovered the foundations of the chancel, both transepts and the north aisle, some coffins and bones. They also found a part of the leg of Monument **M18** – William, Earl Ferrers, that  was re-attached to the effigy.

Clutton's report concluded –

'We subsequently measured the foundations which the excavations had uncovered, and the size of the church appears to have been as follows:- Entire length of the building from east to west, 230 feet. Aisles, in width, 15 feet each. Nave, between the arcades, in width 28 feet; making a total width of nearly 60 feet. Transepts, length from north to south, 88 feet, width 28 feet. Choir, length, 40 feet, width, 28 feet. The buttresses of the choir measure 4 feet in width by five feet in projection; these dimensions apply to the intermediate space between the two base mouldings, of the upper one of which there are no remains. The walls throughout the building have averaged from 3 to 4 feet in thickness.

There is much more to do in the way of excavation; mounds are visible in all directions, and no doubt contain many fragments of wrought stone, which may ultimately throw considerable light upon the architecture of the buildings; until the site has been cleared of these mounds, it is only prudent to suspend an opinion as to what may have been the character of the church when standing.

Unfortunately, the present time of the year is against proceeding with these excavations, and consequently all further investigation will be stopped until the spring of 1850. It is satisfactory to state, that before discontinuing the operations,we discovered the angle of a large building to the south of the choir. This, we think, will turn out to belong to the chapter-house'.

Matthew Bloxam wrote a description in 1864 and produced a 'conjectural' plan based on Clutton's discoveries. It shows a large church of cross plan with north and south aisles to the nave. Certain dimensions are specified, but the proportions of the place drawn, and to which no scale is attached, by no means tally with the sizes mentioned.

The Refectory was parallel to the cloister, instead of following north-south tradition of the Cistercians. The cloister quadrangle was about 112ft from east to west and about 140ft from north to south. The remains of the Refectory (about 96 ft. by 32 ft.) stand in a garden of the Abbey Farm and consist of the east wall and part of the north and south walls standing about 12 ft. high. They include the south stair to the pulpitum, also a section of the west end of the north wall containing the entrance from the cloister. Immediately to the east of this door, on the cloister side can be seen the lavitorium – wash basin (see the Inventory in Appendix G). To the west is the entrance to the former kitchen, all dating from the middle of the 13th century.[5] In 1985 George Wilkie, the Atherstone architect, drew a plan of the abbey site incorporating the drawings of Clutton and Bloxam, the Merevale Estate plans of the farm buildings and the Ordinance survey map. See illustration 'Merevale Abbey – Existing farm buildings over the foundations'.

For some years now a service of Holy Communion has been held in the ruins of the Refectory every year on the Sunday following September 8th, the Feast of the Blessed Virgin Mary.

*The Gate Chapel*

Before the description of the Church, a few words on other Gate Chapels are

*Merevale Abbey Ruins c. 1820 (from the Aylesford Collection, reproduced by kind permission of Birmingham City Archives)*

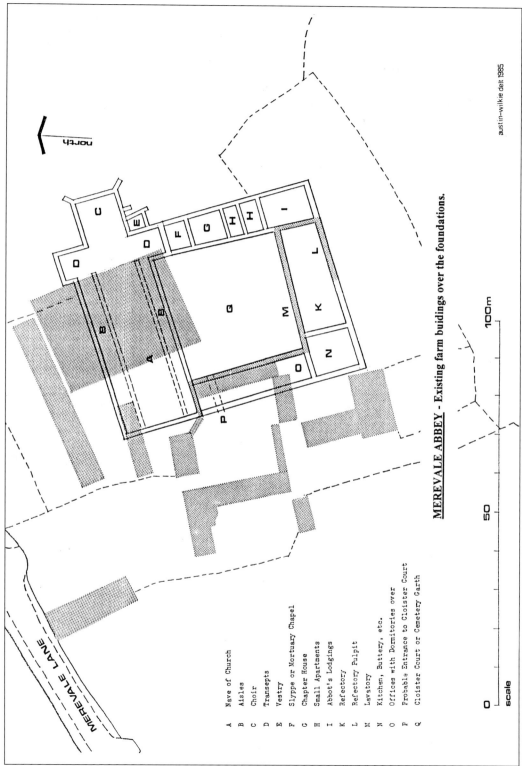

MEREVALE ABBEY - Existing farm buidings over the foundations.

north

MEREVALE LANE

austin-wilkie delt 1985

A    Nave of Church
B    Aisles
C    Choir
D    Transepts
E    Vestry
F    Slyppe or Mortuary Chapel
G    Chapter House
H    Small Apartments
I    Abbot's Lodgings
K    Refectory
L    Refectory Pulpit
M    Lavatory
N    Kitchen, Buttery, etc.
O    Offices with Dormitories over
P    Probable Entrance to Cloister Court
Q    Cloister Court or Cemetery Garth

scale

0        50        100m

*Merevale Abbey – existing farm buildings over the foundations*

necessary, together with a suggested reason for the very unusual nave/chancel proportions at Merevale.

The *Capella ante Portas* – the Chapel outside the Gate – was a specific requirement of the Cistercian rule. Other religious houses sometimes had a gate-chapel, as the conventual church was private. It was used by visitors, their servants, and lay people generally. When a monastery was built in remote places, as were the Cistercian houses, it became even more useful and necessary for the local lay community, however small in number, to have a place of worship. Other surviving Gate Chapels can be seen at Coggeshall, Kirkstead, Hailes, Thame, Rievaulx and Tilty. The chapel at Croxden survived until 1884. There are ruins of chapels at Fountains and Furness. The last is of particular relevance and interest to Merevale. The first reference to the *capella ante portas* at Furness is in 1344 when Bishop Thomas of Lincoln granted an indulgence to those who venerated a statue of the Virgin either 'in the conventual church or the chapel constructed outside the inner gate'. It is not impossible that, as was common enough in these times, a statue of Our Lady, having attained some local repute, became the centre of a small pilgrimage movement in the mid-fourteenth century and was moved by the brethren from the church to the gate chapel.[6] In the south-east corner of the chapel at Furness there is a block of masonry, measuring 28 by 25 inches, built against the east wall. Its original height and its use are both uncertain, but it may have supported an image.[7] It is the author's suggestion that perhaps the south aisle at Merevale was built c.1340 not just to contain the Henore Chantry of 1345, but principally to accommodate the statue of the Virgin. The great number of pilgrims coming to the church in 1361 is well documented, but this was during the *Secunda Pestilencia,* or second wave, of the Black Death. (see monument **M22**) The plague had arrived in England, at Bristol, in 1348. It may well be that the presence of the image, and the subsequent multitude of pilgrims over the years, is the basic reason for the greatly enlarged chancel. Other sources have agreed with this theory.[8] In 1535 the offerings at the image of Our Lady averaged £2 per annum.

The parish church of Our Lady consists of a chancel with side aisles and a nave that has lost its aisles. Modern vestries (1849) occupy the site of the nave south aisle. The development of the plan varies somewhat from that of the normal parish church, the most striking difference being in the length of the chancel (482 ft.) as compared with that of the nave (342 ft.). The nave with aisles dates from about 1240, and there is little doubt that the chancel, on the evidence of its east angles, was originally of the same period. It is possible, as has been suggested by the late Sir William Dugdale, Bt, that the church was erected to serve the monks temporarily while the great abbey church was being rebuilt. This may have been the situation after the disastrous fire at the Abbey in the early 1340s. This would also account for the comparatively abnormal length of the chancel, the small nave being provided for the use of the lay brethren and parishioners.

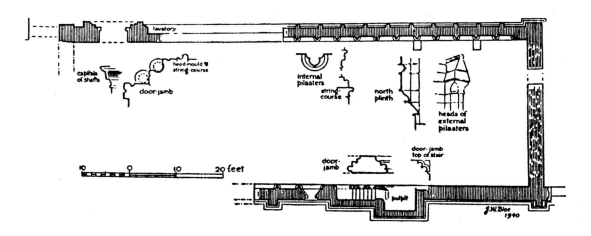

*Plan of the Refectory (reproduced from the V.C.H. Warks. vol. IV, by permission of the General Editor).*

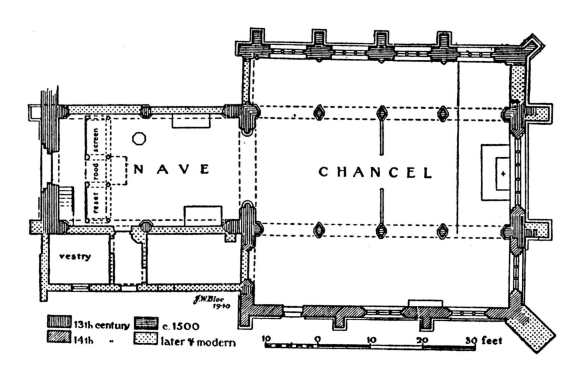

*Plan of the Church of Our Lady (reproduced from the V.C.H. Warks. vol IV, by permission of the General Editor).*

The progressive growth of the plan after the 13th-century is not altogether clear. The jambs and arch of the great east window and the whole of the south aisle date from  c.1340, but the two arcades and the north aisle are of c. 1500.  If the 14th-century work was added to the 13th-century chancel in the usual way, there would have been a contemporary south arcade.  A theory advanced by the late Sir William Dugdale, Bt, is that the church was remodelled after the suppression of the abbey with the use of material from the great abbey church for the south aisle.  If so, re-used material would be found in the arcades and north aisle, but this is not the case; they are good specimens of work of  c. 1500 (although the mouldings in the arcade are peculiarly small) and far better than would be expected from a repatching of  c. 1540 or later.  It is most probable that the south chapel with an arcade was added in the 14th-century, but that the arcade developed weakness and was replaced by the  present arcade to match the north arcade.

The north aisle had a west archway into the 13th-century nave-aisle, which was of the same width, but east wall of the south nave-aisle was left solid, except for an upper window, until, in the 15th-century or subsequently, a narrow archway of re-used 14th-century material was inserted.

There is no evidence as to when the nave-aisles were demolished, but the blocking masonry of the arcades suggests the 18th-century. Around 1850 the vestries were added to the site of the south aisle, and in 1893 much masonry was renewed, the chancel-roof was taken down and reconstructed with the old material and new roofs were supplied to the aisles.

The chancel has an east window of five trefoiled lights and vertical tracery of the 15th-century, the moulded jambs and arch, with hood-moulds on both faces, are of the 14th-century.[9]

The north and south arcades of  c. 1500 are of four 12-ft. bays with moulded piers having three-quarter-found 3 in. shafts on the north and south faces.  The shafts have very small moulded capitals, 4 in., including a 2 in. abacus which passes round the rest of the pier. The bases are also moulded.

The roof is of  pointed wagon-head type and has main arched moulded beams carried by short wall-posts.  The ribs are also moulded and form nine square panels in each side of each bay; the four bays coincide with those of the arcades.  At the intersections are carved conventional foliage bosses.  It is possible that the roof is a little earlier than the arcades and that the side-walls were corbelled inwards to fit its span.

The north aisle (10 ft. wide) has no east window, but at the north end of the wall outside is a vertical straight joint, rising to within four courses of the parapet string-course and suggesting a former archway.  In the north wall are four windows of  c. 1500, each of three plain four-centred lights and tracery in a stilted four-centred head; two quatrefoils above the side-lights are the only piercings that are cusped.[10]

The south aisle (14 ft. wide) has an east and three south windows of mid-14th-century date, each of three trefoiled ogee-headed lights and leaf tracery in two-centred heads with hood-moulds inside and out: the jambs and arches are moulded like those of the chancel east window: the hood-moulds have carved stops – human heads, beasts, etc.  Below the sill of the western south window is a contemporary, walled-up, priests' doorway.

The chancel arch is of the same date as the nave, *c.* 1240. Over it is an oculus, a circular window, which was once glazed. On the chamfered voussoirs facing the chancel can be seen  some remains of painted red decoration.[11] In 1991 the author noticed some faint markings either side of the oculus. As a result of the photographs taken, Dr David Park, of the Conservation of Wall Painting Department, the Courtauld Institute of Art, visited the site. He said that he thought Merevale had one of the earliest Cistercian wall paintings in the country.[12] For a full account of this discovery and Conservation Report, see Appendix E.

The nave has north and south arcades of  two 16 ft. bays of the same date as the chancel arch.  The pillars are octagonal with capitals and bases of similar sections. The arcades are walled up with old rubble-work or rough ashlar, but the blocking on the north side has been cut back to reveal the pillars.  In the blocking of the south-east bay is reset a semi-octagonal moulded bracket supported by a cowled head.   The walls above the arcades are of roughly coursed squared rubble-work, but the top-courses are of modern ashlar replacing Elizabethan brickwork.  In the west wall is a 13th-century doorway. Above is a window of three plain pointed lights under a two-centred head. The gabled wall is of old red sandstone rubble with some remains of a 13th-century plinth like that at the south-east angle of the chancel.  South of the window are traces of a blocked doorway at a low first-floor level, probably a later entrance to a gallery. The buttress in line with the south arcade is modern, of the buttress in line with the north arcade the chamfered lower course of the plinth-base remains.

The nave roof of two bays is like that of the chancel, each bay has twelve panels on each side, no carved bosses remain.  Above the roof near the chancel arch is a modern bell-turret that replaced an earlier one.[13]

Towards the end of the nineteenth century the structural state of the church became a problem. In November 1891 *The Birmingham Mercury* reported that 'after a two foot fall of snow, a visitor could see the unstable appearance of the clustered columns of the north and south aisles. They were tilted and apparently tumbling about in an alarming manner. A few months later the condition of the building had become so serious that it was elaborately shored up, both inside and outside, by timbers as a preliminary to restoration'. This was done in 1893 by Paull and Bickerdike, of London (See Monument **M 16**). The money was raised by local subscription, details of which are in MSS notebooks in the Warwick County Record Office.

In the autumn of 1997 all the tiles were taken off, and the church and the belfry were re-roofed.

*Note on the name Merevale*

It is a result of their required remoteness that the names of Cistercian abbeys were often drawn from the characteristic of the site, especially of the beauty of the place. This is precisely what happened at Merevale: as Dugdale says – 'by reason of such its situation'. It is clear that from an early date the name was interpreted as a hybrid origin and taken to mean 'pleasant valley'. Originally it may have been a purely Latin name – *mira vallis*, 'wonderful valley'. The normal French development from such a name would have been to *vale*. In *vaus* there is a preservation of Old French, which is still found in Rievaulx and Jervaux.[14] In use the name may have been associated with the Old English *myrge* 'merry', and it is possible that Merevale is a translation of *myrge-denu* 'pleasant valley.'[15]

Over the centuries it has been spelt in very many ways, for instance Miravall 1148, Mirevallis 1154, Mirevualle 1157, Mirivaus 1232, Mirivall 1188, Myryvale 1238, Miryvall 1298, Myravale 1561, Miravalle 1656, Mirrival 1733, Merry Vale 1733, Miris Vallibus 1230, Mira Valle 1345, Murivale 1316, Mirewall 1320, Murevall 1461, Merivale 1444, Merevalle 1449, Meryvalle, Merywoll 1523, Meryval 1541, Mearvale 1727.

1    Fergusson 1984, p 5.
2    Dugdale 1656, p 782.
3    Callwood 1985-'90, p 17.
4    Salzman vol IV 1947, p 142.
5    as above, p 143.
6    Dickinson 1967, p63
7    Hope 1900, p 235.
8    Bottomley 1981, p 29.
9    Salzman vol lV 1947, p 144.
10   as above, p 145.
11   as above, p 145.
12   Dr D. Park, personal communication 1 November 1991
13   Salzman vol IV 1945, p 146.
14   Gover 1936, p 87-8.
15   Ekwall 1960, p 322.

# CHAPTER 2

## *THE SUCCESSION OF OWNERS OF THE MEREVALE ESTATE FROM THE DISSOLUTION TO THE PRESENT TIME*

*The Deveraux Family.*

After the Dissolution the Abbey site, in 1541, was granted to Sir Walter Deveraux, Kt, Lord Ferrers, of Chartley, together with the adjacent lands and woods, New House Grange and Pinwell Grange in Leicestershire, and Owstbirn Grange in Warwickshire. In 1551 he received the title of Viscount Hereford.

His youngest son, Sir William Deveraux, Kt., inherited and lived at Merevale, having 'patched up some part of the ruins here, and resided thereon, as I have heard.' (Dugdale 1656). He bequeathed the estate to his wife Joan, for life, and then to Walter, Viscount Hereford, his nephew, and his heirs.  Sir William, then residing at Merevale, obtained permission of the Queen to found a Free Grammar School at Atherstone, together with Thomas Fulner, Merchant, of London, and Amyas Hill, of Atherstone. In 1566 they purchased an estate at Dosthill, and this, with other property, was the endowment of the school. It was established in 1573, by Queen's Letters Patent.  The site of the Augustinian Friary was owned by Amyas Hill and he presented the chapel to the school. This building was later to become the chancel of St Mary's Church, Atherstone. It has been suggested that Michael Drayton, who was born at Hartshill, attended the Grammar School. His earliest work, 'The Harmonie of the Church', a metrical rendering of portions of the scriptures, was published in 1591. Prefixed is a dedicatory epistle,  'To the godly and vertuous Lady, The Lady Jane Devoreux of Merivale,' in which he speaks of the 'bountiful hospitality' he has received from his patroness.

Walter Deveraux, who inherited from his uncle, was born in Carmarthenshire in 1540. He succeeded to the titles of Viscount Hereford and Lord Ferrers when he was nineteen.  On the rebellion of the Northern Earls – against the Protestantism of the Queen – he joined the Lord Admiral and the Earl of Lincoln with a body of troops which put the rebels down. This greatly recommended him to the favour of Queen Elizabeth who, in 1572, honoured him with the Garter, and created him Earl of Essex.  He was afterwards created Governor of Ulster, and died in Dublin in 1576. His armorial bearings (or possibly those of his son Robert) including the insignia of the Garter, were placed in the north aisle of Merevale Church, (see window **n1V – 3d.1**).

He was succeeded by his son, Robert Deveraux, Earl of Essex, who was born in 1567, at Netherwood, in Herefordshire.  At the age of nine he inherited the earldom, and heavy debts. He was left in the guardianship of Cecil, Lord Burleigh. When he

*Robert Deveraux, 2rd Earl of Essex
(1567-1601)*

*Robert Deveraux, 3rd Earl of Essex (1592-1686).
General of the Parliamentary Army*

was twelve he went to Trinity College, Cambridge, and at seventeen he was introduced at Court. Essex's good looks and charm , which considerably outranked his talents, fascinated Elizabeth. In 1585, he accompanied Leicester, whom his mother had married, to Holland, and distinguished himself at the battle of Zutpen. On his return he was made Master of the Horse, in place of the Earl of Leicester, and advanced to the post of High Steward.  In 1588, when the Queen assembled an army at Tilbury to resist the Spanish invasion, the Earl of Essex was appointed General of the Horse, and was soon after decorated with the Order of the Garter. These rapid promotions fuelled his pride and vanity and laid the seeds of his downfall. Throughout the 1590s he exploited the Queen's affection and acted as a loose cannon in politics, seeking power and glory. His military endeavours were showy, expensive and progressively more unsuccessful: the seige of Rouen (1591), the sack of Calais (1596),  the abortive Azores raid on the Spanish treasure fleet (1597), and most disastrously, the expedition to Ireland as Lord Lieutenant (1599-1600). Essex squandered the best equipped English army yet sent to Ireland, signing a truce with the rebel Tyrone. Earlier he had made a private marriage with the only daughter of Sir Francis Walsingham, with which the Queen was not well pleased.

Prior to leaving for Ireland an embarrassing confrontation took place at Nonsuch Palace. At a private Council some dispute arose, and Essex contemptuously turned his back on the Queen. Sir Walter Raleigh said that he told her that 'her ideas were as crooked as her carcass'. Elizabeth, stung beyond endurance, struck him a violent blow on the ear, and bade him go and be hanged. Clasping his sword, Essex swore that he neither could nor would put up with such an affront, which he would not have taken from King Henry VIII himself.  Essex was induced to make some apology, but the ill-feeling produced by this scene was never completely effaced on either side. On returning to England he was suspended from all his offices except that of Master of the Horse. He afterwards took some dislike to the Queen, and indulged in further disrespectful remarks towards her. Ultimately he formed a conspiracy against the Queen and Government and tried to get support from the citizens of London. He was apprehended and committed to the Tower; his guilt was easily proved, and sentence was pronounced.  The Queen was reluctant to sign the warrant for his execution, but she ultimately did so.  He was executed in the Tower on February 25, 1601, aged 34.  His mother, the Countess of Leicester, often lived at Drayton Manor, and he sometimes visited her there.

Essex's character is a simple one. He was devoid of nearly every quality of which statesmen are made. Frank, passionate, and impulsive as a schoolboy, he had no control whatever over his feelings, and at a court like Elizabeth's, split into warring factions, his attempt to make a great political position by force of his personal character was doomed to failure. (*Roberto Deveraux*, one of Donizetti's lesser known operas, of 1837, was performed at the Player's Theatre, London, in 1998).

He was succeeded by his son, Robert Deveraux, Earl of Essex, born in 1592. When he was ten he went to Merton College, Oxford.   James I restored him to hereditary honours in 1603. When he was fourteen he married Lady Frances Howard, daughter of the Earl of Suffolk. Neither this, nor his second marriage, to the daughter of Sir William Paulet, lasted very long. When the Scottish Covenanters rebelled in 1639, he was made Lieutenant-General of the Army. In 1641 he was created Lord Chamberlain of the Household and in July 1642 he accepted the post of General of the Parliamentary Army.  He fought with the King in person at Edge Hill. In 1644 he marched into Cornwall  where he was followed by the King's forces. His infantry later capitulated and he, with his principal officers, escaped by sea. In April 1645 he resigned his commission but Parliament voted that he should be raised to the Dukedom and have an annual grant of ten thousand pounds, but neither of these took place.  He died of a sudden illness in September 1646 at Essex House in the Strand, and was buried at Westminster Abbey with a public funeral, leaving his two sisters as his co-heirs.

He lived principally at Chartley, and occasionally at Drayton Manor, the former residence of his grandmother, the Countess of Leicester, and over his pew, in the old church at Drayton, were carved his initials, coronet, and supporters, with the date 1620. The manor of Merevale seems to have been to have passed to the younger sister, Frances, who married William Seymour, Marquess of Hertford, and to have been sold by them, probably in 1649, to Edward Stratford.  However the actual Abbey site was not included in the sale, presumably because of the various ancestors of the Ferrers family buried there, but was transferred some years later.[1]

### The Stratford Family.
In 1615 Robert Stratford of London owned the rectory of Ansley, together with other possessions formerly belonging to the nuns of Polesworth. By his will of the same year, he gave 20s. yearly to be spent on bread on Good Friday for poor persons in Ansley, and left his property to his nephew, Edward Stratford, when he became 28 years old.  Robert Stratford died in August 1615.[b] Edward Stratford purchased the Merevale  estate probably in 1649.

With the communion plate of Ansley is one small salver inscribed – 'Mr Robert Stratford did give to enlarge this coup three pounds; then C. wardens Daniel Oughton, Thomas Kennon, 1619'.

In 1658-9 a fine was levied of one messuage, two cottages, three gardens, two orchards, 20 acres of land, 10 acres of meadow, 100 acres of pasture, 7 acres of wood, and common pasture for all cattle in Bretshall, Ansley, Hartshill and Stockingford. The plaintiff was William Thornton, and Thomas White and others were the Deforcients ('landowners' who had no legal right). In 1661  William Thornton conveyed it to John Stratford, Esq., wool merchant, of Horston (Oaston) Grange, in the parish of Nuneaton, (about a mile from Nuneaton, to the north of the Hinckley road). His descendant, Francis Stratford of Merevale, in 1732, exchanged it for a spring wood called Hoare Park, in the hamlet of Bentley and parish of Shustoke, in consideration of £180, with John Ludford, Esq.

Mary, the daughter of John Stratford, Esq., married Mr Combes, who is buried in Nuneaton Church. On the monument there is the inscription, translated, – 'To the memory of Mary, wife of Richard Combes, and daughter of John Stratford. Edward Stratford, her first born, erected this tomb. She numbered nine children, only five of whom survive; the rest this earth covers. She departed hence on 12th day of June, in the year of our Lord 1668. Reader, mark my end; in a short time you will be as I am'.

Abigail, another daughter of Mr Stratford was also buried here, with the inscription, translated, – 'Sacred to the memory of Antony Trotman, who was descended from a noble and ancient Wiltshire family. He married Abigail, the daughter of Squire Stratford, late of Merevale, (near whose remains their families now lie), on the 12th of August, 1662. She was eleven times a mother, leaving nine survivors. When he had lived one and forty years with honour and illustrious worth, and with usefulness to his spouse and his numerous friends, and accessible to all, (joys which have an end terminate with the end,) he left a widowed couch on the 12th day of August, 1703. She, when her better half was snatched away, behaved with temperate grief and faith, and followed her deceased husband, after fulfilling with warm affection her duties towards those living; a survivor of her husband, and two years beyond, she calmly fell asleep in Christ May the 8th, 1705. Their son, moved by just piety, erected this marble'.

In Ansley Church is an achievement of John Stratford, Esq., of Merevale, who was buried in the chancel 6th September, 1724. Argent, a lion rampant, upon five bars, sable impaling vert, three horses argent. Crest, an armed arm proper.

Over the chancel door, before Mr Stratford white-washed it, in about 1736, at the request of Thomas Ebdell, vicar, was this inscription – "Mr Robert Stratford, gent., buried 30th August, 1615, gave 20s yearly for ever to be given in bread to the poor of Ansley, besides other gifts which he gave to the church. N.B. The bread was always given to the poor of Ansley on Good Friday by Mr Stratford, of Merevale, and his father before him"[2]

Thomas Simmonds lived at Merevale Hall in 1744. A mural monument in Mancetter church has this inscription – "In hopes of a joyful resurrection to the life immortal, beneath this monument lies interred the body of Mrs Elizabeth Simmonds, late wife of Thomas Simmonds, of Merevale Abbey, in this county, gent. She departed this life in the true faith and fear of Almighty God on February 14th, 1744, aged 44 years, 2 months, and 28 days.

Since every one who lives is born to die,
And none can boast sincere felicity,
With equal mind what happens let us bear,
Nor grieve too much for things beyond our care.
Like pilgrims to the appointed place we tend,
The world's an inn, and death the journey's end.

*Sir William Dugdale, Kt., Garter King of Arms (1605-1686).*

On a marble tablet underneath – "Thomas Simmond, a gent., died the 5th November, 1747, aged 46 years." Thomas Simmonds and Francis Stratford were joint patrons of Merevale Church, each appointing the incumbent alternately.

Francis Stratford, Esq., the last of that name that owned this estate, was buried at Merevale in 1762.  His widow, Anna, who held it for life, died in 1779. (See Monument **M30**) There are also two hatchments, **M7** and **M15**, in memory of Francis and Anna Stratford respectively.

In 1749 the rectory of Ansley became vested in Richard Geast, Esq., as trustee and (in right of his wife) heir of Francis Stratford, Esq., as also the Merevale estates at the death of his widow in 1779.

*Sir William Dugdale Kt and Family.*
James Dugdale lived in Clitheroe, Lancashire, in the latter part of the sixteenth century. He came of a family which had been well-established there. His son John went to Oxford, taking his M.A. degree, and afterwards was employed in an official capacity at the University.  Upon his leaving Oxford John decided to live in Warwickshire, taking a long lease on the Rectory at Shustoke, near Coleshill.  Here his famous, and only, son was born on the 12th September, 1605. His mother was Elizabeth, daughter of Arthur Swynfen, of Swynfen, a member of an old Staffordshire family.

William Dugdale received his earliest education from Thomas Sibley, curate of Nether Whitacre, and later went to the Free School at Coventry, his education being completed at home under his father's supervision.  His father, who was in a poor state of health, wished to see his son married before his death, so, on the 17th March, 1622, at the early age of sixteen, he married Margery, daughter of John Huntbache, of Seawall, Staffordshire.  John Dugdale died in 1624, and his son went to live on the estate at Fillongley which had been left to him. The following year he returned to Shustoke, having sold his property at Fillongley, and purchased the estate of Blythe Hall from Sir Walter Aston.

William Dugdale began to make a study of history and antiquities and made the acquaintance of several well informed men, such as Sir Simon Archer and William Burton, the historian of Leicestershire.  By 1638 he had collected a quantity of historical material relating to Warwickshire, and going to London with Sir Simon, he was introduced to various influential men with like interests, among them Sir Christopher Hatton and Sir Henry Spelman.  The result was that later in the same year he was created a Pursuivant at Arms Extraordinary. In the following year he was raised to the post of Rouge Croix Pursuivant-in-Ordinary, and made good use of his opportunities as a herald to increase his store of knowledge, all the national records being now at his disposal.

In 1642 Charles I summoned Dugdale to join his forces, and the following year he fought at Edgehill. Blythe Hall was confiscated by Parliament in due course, but was redeemed by a fine of £168.  Among the duties assigned to Dugdale as a herald during the early part of the Civil War was to demand the surrender of Banbury and Warwick Castles. In the former case his demand was successful, but in the latter he was effectually defied by Sir Edward Peyto of Chesterton.

King Charles created him Chester Herald in 1644. Though he had been far from idle in historical research during the war, he now had more time at his disposal. In fact from 1642 to 1644 when he was with the Court at Oxford he found time for study at the Bodleian and the college libraries. *The Antiquities of Warwickshire* was published in 1656 at his own expense. This work, the most famous of county

*William Stratford Dugdale (1828-1882).*

histories, would have been accounted a life's work for an ordinary man, but Dugdale was not an ordinary man, and the book was only one of several colossal works which were the product of his brain and industry. In 1658 appeared his *History of St Paul's Cathedral,* the massive *Monasticon Anglicanum* being published at intervals between 1652 and1673, and *The Baronage of England* in 1675.

At the Restoration Dugdale became Norroy King of Arms, and in 1677 Garter Principal King of Arms and also knighted by Charles II. He died on February 10th, 1686, at Blythe Hall, aged eighty. His wife had died in 1681, after a married life of fifty-nine years. Both are buried in Shustoke Church, where their tomb successfully withstood the fire which practically destroyed the church in 1886.

Sir William Dugdale had many daughters, but only one son, who succeeded him at Blythe. John Dugdale followed in his father's footsteps as a herald and in 1675 was appointed Windsor Herald in the place of his brother-in-law, Elias Ashmole. He later became Norroy King of Arms and was knighted by James II. Sir John Dugdale, who was born in 1628, died at Coventry in 1700, and was buried at Shustoke. By his wife, Mary, daughter of Alexander Baker, of New Windsor, he left a son and a daughter, and by his second wife, Elisabeth, daughter of Alderman Thomas Pidgeon, of Coventry, one daughter. He was succeeded by his son, William Dugdale, of Blythe Hall.

William Dugdale married (in 1686) Judith, daughter of John Gough, of Bushbury, Staffordshire, and was succeeded at his death in 1714 by his son, John Dugdale, who following the family tradition became Mowbray Herald Extraordinary. He died without issue in 1749, and so ended the male line of Sir William Dugdale's descendants. However John Dugdale had a sister Jane, who, in 1722 married Richard Geast, of Handsworth. Her eldest son, Richard, succeeded to the Dugdale estates, under the will of his uncle, John Dugdale. He was a barrister, who married in 1767 Penelope, eldest daughter of Francis Stratford of Merevale. In 1799 he assumed the name and arms of Dugdale. He died in 1806, leaving one son and three daughters, one of whom married William Dilke, of Maxstoke Castle.

Richard Geast Dugdale's only son and heir was Dugdale Stratford Dugdale (1773-1836), who succeeded to Merevale Hall, which became the chief home of the family. From 1802-1830 he was M.P. for North Warwickshire. By his first wife, the Hon. Charlotte Curzon, daughter of Asseton, first Viscount Curzon, he left an only son and heir, William Stratford Dugdale. (See memorial **M33** and hatchment **M38**).

William Stratford Dugdale was born at Merevale on 1st April, 1800, (also see window **s111**). He was educated at Westminster School and Christ Church, Oxford. In 1830 he succeeded his father as M.P. for North Warwickshire. He lost his seat at the election immediately following the passing of the Reform Bill. However the Government only lasted for ten months, and at the subsequent election he regained the seat and held it until 1847. In 1827 he married Harriet Ella Portman, youngest daughter of Edward Berkeley Portman, Esq., of Bryanstone House, Blandford,

Dorset, and sister of Viscount Portman. More often than not past generations of Dugdales had only one son, but in this case there were seven sons, in addition to three daughters, of whom six sons and two daughters survived. He rebuilt Merevale Hall to the design of Edward Blore, assisted by Henry Clutton, from 1835 to 1840. With Clutton as architect he built Baddesley Church in 1848 and the Gate House and the Archway at Merevale in 1849. Together they did some excavation of the Abbey ruins in 1849 and restored Merevale Church. He was Churchwarden at St George's, Hanover Square. He continued the mining enterprise started by his father in the last two decades of the eighteenth Century. In 1851 he sank two new shafts at Baddesley and set up the modern mining business that lasted until the Coal Board closed the pit in 1985. He maintained an interesting diary which is in the library at Merevale Hall. Mr Dugdale died at Blythe Hall on 15th September, 1871, and was succeeded at Merevale and Blythe by his eldest son, another William Stratford Dugdale. His third son, John Stratford Dugdale, was Recorder of Birmingham, Chairman of the Warwickshire County Council, and M.P. for the Nuneaton Division of Warwickshire (1886-1892). He lived at Blythe Hall, (see memorial **M40**). The fourth son, Henry Charles Geast Dugdale, was a soldier, and Colonel in the Rifle Brigade. The sixth Edward Stratford Dugdale, lived in Scotland, a naval officer, and died in 1931 at the age of eighty-five. Adelaide, the second daughter, was a god-daughter of Queen Adelaide. She married Arthur Wellesley, Viscount Peel, a son of Sir Robert Peel, and a notable Speaker of the House of Commons.[3]

The second William Stratford Dugdale (see window **s11**) was born in 1828. He was educated at Eton and Balliol College, Oxford where he was one of the earliest pupils and friends of Benjamin Jowett, (Master of Balliol College 1870-1893). Jowett occasionally visited Merevale in the late 1870s and he was godfather to the present Sir William Dugdale's father. He got first class honours and was for a short time a tutor at Balliol. He translated Dante – one of his specialities was Italian. He became a Barrister-at-Law but because of his bad stammer he did not practise. He was Chairman of the Metropole Hotel, Brighton, when it opened in the late 1860s.

In 1871 he married Alice Frances Trevelyan. She was the youngest daughter of Sir Charles Edward Trevelyan, Bt, of Wallingford, Northumberland, and a niece of Lord Macaulay, the historian, (see memorial **M28**). He was High Sheriff for the County in 1876. On the morning of 2nd May, 1882 a disastrous fire occurred at Baddesley Pit trapping nine miners. Mr Dugdale went underground with the rescue team in a heroic attempt to rescue them. In a further explosion he sustained severe burns from which, seven days later, he died. When he was brought home he said 'I shall die, but I do not care what I suffer, as it is for the good of my people'. In fact all twenty-four men in the rescue operation later died from their injuries. At the top of the incline road, in the Stratford mine, there is a memorial stone plaque set in the coal face which reads 'W.S.D. May 2nd 1882'. The pit is now closed.

He was succeeded by his elder son, William Francis Stratford Dugdale, who was born in 1872. He was educated at Eton and Balliol College, Oxford. He was a magistrate when he was only 22, was elected to the County Council in 1904, and was Chairman from 1934 to 1947. For many years he was Chairman of the Finance Committee and played a notable part in carrying out changes in the county administration. He served as High Sheriff of Warwickshire in 1911-12 and as Vice-Lieutenant from 1939 to 1964. He was created a Baronet in 1936. Amongst many other offices Sir William was a Governor and Trustee of Rugby School, a Life Trustee of Shakespeare's Birthplace, and the vice-president and, later, president of the Dugdale Society from 1925 until his death. He was a member of the Roxburge Club and devoted considerable time and effort to the publication of *The Restoration of the Beauchamp Chapel at St Mary's Collegiate Church Warwick 1674-1742* which he presented to the members in 1956. He was formerly Chairman and Managing Director of Baddesley Collieries Ltd. He died on Easter Sunday 1965 at the age of 92.

Sir William was a great lover of his county and its history and he had a particularly wide range of historical and antiquarian knowledge. He was understandably and justly proud of his ancestor, the famous herald and historian of Warwickshire. He will long be remembered for his dignified upright bearing, his extraordinary memory and his fund of reminiscences.

His eldest son is the present Sir William Dugdale, Bt, to whom this account of the Dugdale family is heavily indebted.

---

1    Stephen 1964, p 889.
2    Bartlett 1791, p 134.
3    Burnam 1934, p 54.

# CHAPTER 3

## *CATALOGUE OF THE WINDOWS*

### Numbering of the Windows

The windows, and the panels of glass in them, have been numbered in accordance with the classification recommended by the Corpus Vitrearum Medii Aevii - the C.V.M.A. This is the body which, under the auspices of the Comité Internationale d'Histoire de l'Art and the patronage of the Union Academique Internationale, are currently publishing substantial works on the major medieval glass in Europe.

Under this system the east window is window **I. The** windows in the north aisle, **n11, n111, n1V, nV** follow on, going westwards, and then those in the south aisle, **s11, s111, s1V, sV, sV1**. The west window is **w1**. The panels and details within a panel are described starting at the bottom left-hand corner of each window. The numbers designate the row, working upwards, and the letters show the panel within a row, working to the right. The glass in the main lights have numbers and lower case letters. In the tracery lights upper case letters are used and the order is reversed. The division between the lower lights and the tracery lights is usually the springing line, that is the level at which an arch springs from its supports. It follows that **3c** in **1** is the third panel in the third row in window **1** (The figure of Christ), and **A2** in **n11** the top right-hand angel in window **n11**. A noteworthy piece of glass within a panel has its own number; **C1.12** in **1** is on the north side at the top of window **1** (a seagull).

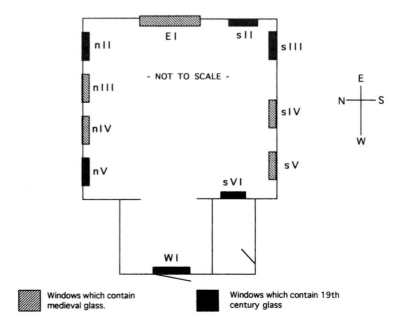

*Plan of windows*

## **Window 1**

h. 5.76 m. w. 3.84 m.

## THE MAIN LIGHTS

The Jesse Window

The bottom row of the main lights, depicting the five Kings Rehoboam, Manesseh, Jehosaphat, Jehoram and Asa, are mostly nineteenth century glass by Ward and Hughes. (See Appendix C – *Victorian Glass Manufacturers*).  They were put in the window about 1872 when the medieval Jesse glass was restored. The rest of the glass in the main lights  is around 1330-1340.

For a full account of the history of the Merevale Jesse, other medieval Jesse windows, and the origin and iconography of the subject see Chapter 5 – *The Tree of Jesse and Jesse Windows*.

**1a**    King Rehoboam
His right hand holds a sword and his left hand the end of the scroll, which falls over his left knee. The text, in black letter, reads:

## RE | HOBOAM  REX

The cloak is green with  blue facings, the tunic is crimson. The panel is mostly modern incorporating a  few scraps of original  glass. The figure is completely modern and has been copied from **2c**, Solomon.

He was the son of King Solomon, but not so wise a leader and the people rebelled. The ten  northern tribes  made  him  their King. Only Judah and Benjamin stayed loyal to Rehoboam. From this time  the northern kingdom was known as Israel, and the southern kingdom as Judah. Rehoboam was defeated by Egypt, and for much of his reign was  at  war with Jeroboam.

**1a.1**  An owl in profile facing right, the head frontal, white glass touched yellow stain.

**1a.2**  A bird facing left, the head facing right.

Borders
**1a.3**  Fragments of medieval glass in both borders. (14th-16thC)

**1b**    King Manesseh
His left hand holds a sceptre, his right hand points to the scroll that reads, in black letter:

MANESSES : REX

The cloak is pale claret coloured and the tunic a deeper tone of the same colour. The panel is mostly modern, copied from **2d**, King Hezekiah.
He was Joseph's eldest son and King of Judah for fifty-five years. He led the nation astray, introducing all kinds of idolatry. He was taken prisoner by the Assyrians but later returned to Jerusalem, and to God.

**1b.1**    Bird in profile facing left. White glass touched yellow stain. (16thC)

Borders
**1b.2**    Fragments of medieval glass in both borders.(14th-16thC)

**1c**    King Jehosaphat
His right hand holds a sceptre. The scroll reads, in black letter:

† JAPHAPHET

The cloak is crimson and the tunic ochre. The panel is mostly modern and the figure completely modern., the cartoon copied from **3d**, Josias.

Son of King Asa, he was king of Judah from 870 to 848 B.C. He was a strong king who destroyed idols, and ensured that his subjects obeyed God's law. He improved the legal system and appointed judges in the major towns.

**1c.1**    Bird in profile facing left. White glass touched with yellow stain.

Borders
**1c.2**    Fragments of medieval and modern glass both borders. Type A. (14th-16thC)

**1d**    King Jehoram
As Rehoboam, his right hand holds a sword and his left hand the end of the scroll, which hangs over his left knee. The text, in black letter reads:

JORAM : REX

The cloak is crimson and the tunic ochre. The panel is mostly modern, the figure completely modern, the cartoon copied from **2c**, Solomon.

King of Judah 848 – 841 B.C. after his father, Ahab. Elijah warned that  he would die from a terrible disease because he had  murdered his six brothers and encouraged his subjects to worship. He  was murdered by Jehu who was anointed king by Elisha,  and was told to wipe out all King  Ahab's and Jezebel's descendants. Jehu did so.

**1d.1** An owl in profile facing left, the head frontal. White glass touched with yellow stain.(14thC).

**1d.2** A bird in profile facing left, the head facing right.(14thC).

Borders.
**1d.3** Fragments of medieval glass in both borders.(14th-16thC).

**1e** <u>King Asa</u>
As Manasseh, the right hand holds a sceptre, and the  left hand points to the scroll. The cloak is green, the  tunic blue and  claret. The panel is mostly modern. The figure is completely modern and is a copy of **2d**, King Hezekiah. The  inscription  however  is  original  and  is  made  up  from two inscriptions in black letter:

# ASA IES: REX.

Dr Newton states that this inscription is the only  medieval one amongst the five Ward and Hughes restored  figures, but it is difficult to see why he does not also include the scroll of Mannesseh as of the same date.
King of Judah 911-870 B.C. He won a great victory when a huge Ethiopian army, led by Zerah, attacked Judah.

**1e.1** Bird in profile facing left. White glass touched with yellow stain. (14thC)

Borders.
**1e.2** Fragments of medieval glass in both borders. (14th-16thC)

**2a** <u>Prophet Malachi</u> in the coils of the vine, full length , facing three- quarter right looking upwards, he grasped the stem with his right hand. In his left hand is a scroll  inscribed in black letter:-

# MALC I HIA I S PROFETE.

The head and hands are in  white  glass,  the hair and beard touched with yellow stain. He wears  an ochre cloak  over a murrey tunic. The hem  and the tunic are patterned against a fragmentary ground of blue and ruby pieces diapered with a foliage design, as in the tracery lights. (14th C.)   The last of the Old Testament prophets, about mid-fifth century B.C. His prophecy about the messenger who shall prepare the way of the Lord (Malachi iii. 10) is applied to John the Baptist, whilst the reference to the 'pure offering ' (Malachi i. 11) is taken in Christian tradition as a prophecy of the Eucharist.

The head, and a dozen small pieces, seem at some stage to have been re-leaded with the painting on the outside. This was probably done when the window was reconstructed, in order to balance the appearance. This is perhaps why these pieces of glass have deteriorated so badly .

**2a.1**   A letter '**P**' scratched on the glass. A glazier's position mark – see *Glossary*, and also the chapter on *Stained and Painted Glass.* There is a very similar P mark of the early 14thC in Wells Cathedral. (14thC)

Borders

**2a.2**   A dragon, biting itself. (14thC)

**2a.3**   A dragon's head. (14thC)

**2a.4**   A dragon's head, biting its wing. (14thC)

**2a.5**   A lion passant guardant in yellow glass has been inserted adjacent to the end of the scroll.

**2b**   King David

Represented seated akimbo playing the harp, facing three-quarters right. He plucks the harp strings with his right hand and holds a sceptre in his left. The ochre crown is separately leaded, his hands and face are in flesh coloured glass. He wears a green cloak over a murrey tunic, the  hems are patterned. His ochre shoes are diapered. The harp is in yellow stain and has a monkey's head ornament at the top. Fragments of a blue ground diapered with a foliage design as **3a**. (14thC) Sarah Brown, of the R.C.H.M.E., suggests that this king appears to be on a smaller scale, and perhaps by a different artist.

The first king of the Judean dynasty. After his victory over Goliath, the Philistine giant, he was promoted by  King Saul and married his daughter. He subsequently provoked Saul's jealously and went into exile. On Saul's death he set himself up as king. He made Jerusalem his   capital and reigned there for thirty-three years. He restored the Ark to  the city,  planned the building of the Temple, and broke the ascendancy  of the Philistines. Traditionally regarded  as the author of the Psalms. Customarily portrayed with his harp. Died c. 970 B.C. He was the father of King Solomon.

**2b.1`** A bird in profile facing right (14thC)

**2b.2** A squirrel, identical with **3c.4**.

Borders
**2b.3** A dragon biting its wing (14thC)

**2b.4** A dragon biting itself (14thC)

**2b.5** The eye of a dragon (14thC)

**2c** King Solomon
Represented seated facing three-quarters right, the head in profile, the vine stem forming an oval about him. He holds a sword in his right hand, a scroll in his left hand is inscribed, in black letter:

† SAC | LOMO | N : REX.

Ochre crown separately leaded. The head (modern restoration) and gloved hands are in white glass. The figure's diaper is much broken and disarranged, with pieces of an ochre cloak with a patterned hem and a piece  of green patterned drapery. The sword is white with a yellow stain  rib. Fragments of a blue ground with a foliage design as **2b**. (14thC.)
     The impression given in 1 Kings 1-11 is of an  Oriental  despot, honoured for  his  wealth  and  wisdom.  His  reign  marked  the  zenith of ancient Israel's prosperity. The  levies  and  forced  labour  that  he  imposed  to complete  his grandiose building schemes in Jerusalem, including the Temple, resulted in the discontent that, after his death, led to the  secession of the ten northern tribes.

**2c.1** The name **'John Smith'** (done in the 18thC ?) scratched in the centre of Solomon's right hand (14thC).

**2c.2** An owl facing right, the head frontal. White glass touched with yellow stain (14thC) .

**2c.3** Bird in profile facing left, white glass touched with yellow stain (14thC)

Borders
**2c.4** Alternating fleur-de-lys and roses. Type A. (14thC) .

**2d**    <u>King Hezekiah</u>
Represented seated, with his left leg drawn up, facing three-quarters left, the vine stem forms an oval about him. He is crowned and holds a sceptre in his left hand. A scroll in his right hand is inscribed in black letter:

† 𝔈𝔷𝔢𝔠𝔥𝔦 | 𝔞𝔰  𝔯𝔢𝔵.

Crown in yellow stain, separately leaded, the head and white gloves are in white glass. He wears a murrey cloak with green patterned bands at the shoulders and a ruby tunic. The hems of the cloak and tunic are patterned. His green hose and ochre shoes are richly diapered. His sceptre is gold with finial apex. Fragments of a blue ground with a foliage design as **3a** (14thC)
    King of Judah 716-687 B.C. He organised a national campaign to destroy everything do with idol worship. During his reign the northern kingdom of Israel was conquered by Assyria. He cut a rock tunnel to ensure a water supply to Jerusalem in the event of seige.

**2d.1**   Bird in profile facing left. White glass touched with yellow stain. (14thC).

<u>Borders</u>
**2d.2**   Fragments of medieval glass in both borders (14th-16thC)

**2e**    <u>Prophet Moses</u>
Represented standing in the coils of the vine, full length facing three-quarters left, the head turned to the right. He holds the tablets of the law in his left hand, and a scroll in his right hand is inscribed in black letter:

𝔪𝔬𝔶𝔰 | 𝔢𝔰𝔭𝔯 | 𝔬𝔣𝔢𝔱𝔢

The head and hands are in flesh-coloured glass, the horns are blue. He wears a green cloak over an ochre tunic, the hems are patterned green. The tunic has been slightly disarranged. The tablets of the law are ruby red. (14thC) . Pieces of blue ground as in **3a**.
    He was the Founder and law-giver of Israel. He led the Hebrews out of their bondage in Egypt. During their journey across the desert they often rebelled against him, but by his intercession they were given manna for food, and the Ten Commandments. He was granted a sight of the promised land and died in Moab. Moses figures prominently in Christian tradition. At the Transformation he appears as the representative of the Law.
    Moses is consistently portrayed in medieval art as having horns. In the Vulgate, Exodus xxxiv.35 reads 'Qui videbant faciem egredient is Moses este cornuram', meaning that light shone from his head, or face, perhaps as in a

halo. The word 'cornuram' was probably mistranslated as meaning 'horned' and in this way the tradition arose of portraying Moses with actual horns. This literal interpretation by artists goes back as far as the eleventh century.

**2e.1**  The upper half of  the small head of a Saint (?), facing three-quarters left has been inserted between the figure's right hand and the scroll. In white glass and rather decayed. (14thC.)

Borders
**2e.2**  Head of a Dragon  (14thC)

**2e.3**  Fine dragon biting its tail (14thC)

**2e.4**  Large hawk (14thC)

**3a**  Prophet Zephaniah
Represented standing in the coils of the vine, full length, facing three-quarters right looking upwards. He grasps the vine stem with both hands, a scroll runs upward from his right hand inscribed, in black letter:

SOPH | JAS PROF | ETE |.

He wears a white cloak, which also covers his head, and an ochre tunic. The hems of these garments are patterned and the tunic is crossed by parallel bands. The head and the hands are in flesh-coloured glass. The left eye and part of the beard is decayed. Against a ruby ground  that bears a running foliage design reserved on a ground of black enamel.

Zephaniah was a prophet in Judah about 600 B.C. He forecast the approaching judgement of all nations in the Day of the Lord. The opening words of the 'Dies irae' are taken from the Vulgate version of Zephaniah 1:15.

**3a.1**  An owl. in profile facing left, the head frontal. White glass touched yellow stain. (14thC)

Borders
**3a.2**  A dragon biting its wing (14thC)

**3a.3**  A dragon (14thC)

**3a.4**  A fine dragon biting its tail (14thC)

**3a.5**  A large hawk. Type C. (14thC)

**3b**    <u>A King</u>
Represented seated akimbo facing right, the head turned three-quarters left, the vine stem forms an oval frame about him.

Crowned, holding a sword in his right hand, he wears a ruby cloak with a patterned hem.

The face is in flesh-coloured glass, the yellow crown is separately leaded. Against a blue ground diapered with continuous circles, each containing a quatrefoil, reserved on a black enamel ground.

This figure has been disturbed. The feet and left hand are missing. The cloak is incomplete, the tunic has been replaced by pieces of plain glass and broken pieces of drapery. (14thC.)

**3b.1**  A small monkey seated facing three-quarters left, white glass (?), rather decayed. (14thC)

**3b.2**  Upper half of a small head of a youth facing three-quarters right, in white glass, rather decayed. (14thC)

<u>Borders</u>
**3b.3**  Fragments of medieval glass in both borders. (14thC).

**3c**    <u>A Panel of Fragments</u>
**3c.1**  An incomplete frontal figure of Christ displaying the wounds of the Passion, the head and raised arms in white glass with touches of yellow stain. The eyes are oblique. Inserted from a 15th. C. window into a panel of otherwise 14thC. glass.

**3c.2**  Fragmentary pieces of ochre and green coloured drapery, part of a patterned hem in ruby glass. (14thC)

**3c.3**  Small pieces of diapered glass. (14thC)

**3c.4**  A squirrel seated on its hind legs eating a nut, profile facing right, white glass (?), rather decayed. (14thC)

**3c.5**  The hand of a figure , a Prophet ?, facing left, grasping the vine stem. (14thC)

**3c.6**  Bird in profile facing left. White glass touched with yellow stain. (14thC)

**3c.7**  A hawk facing right, head turned looking left.(14thC)

<u>Borders</u>
**3c.8**  Alternating fleur-de-lys and rosettes in diamond. Type A. (14thC)

**3d**    <u>King Josiah</u>
Represented facing three-quarters left, the vine stem forms an oval about him. Crowned, holding a sceptre in his right hand, a scroll running downwards from his left hand is inscribed, in black letter:

𝕵 𝖘𝕵 | 𝕬𝖘 : | 𝕽𝕰𝖃 :

Yellow crown, separately leaded, the head and gloved hands are in white glass. He wears an ochre cloak over a murrey tunic, the hems are patterned. His green hose and ruby shoes are richly diapered. The sceptre is ruby with a finial top in yellow stain. Against a blue ground, diapered with a foliage design as **B1** below also pieces diapered with circles. (14thC)
    King of Judah in 640 B.C., at the age of eight. He was a humane and moral leader. He ordered the rebuilding of the temple at Jerusalem. He was killed in battle against the Egyptians when he was thirty-nine.

**3d.1**    A hawk in profile facing left. White glass touched with yellow stain. (14thC)

<u>Borders</u>
**3d.2**    Fragments of medieval glass in both borders.

**3e**    <u>Prophet Isaiah</u>
Represented standing in the coils of the vine, full length facing three-quarters left looking upwards, he grasps the stem with his left hand. In his veiled right hand he holds a scroll inscribed in black letter:

𝖀𝖘𝕬 | 𝕵𝕬𝖘 : 𝕻𝕽𝕺𝕱𝕰 | 𝕿𝕰.

The head and the hands are in white glass. He wears an ochre tunic, the hems are patterned. The tunic is decayed and semi-opaque. Fragments of a blue ground diapered with a foliage design. (14thC)
    An important Hebrew prophet, he was influential at the court of the kings of Judah especially in foreign affairs. Called to the prophetic office c. 740 B.C., he continued his work until the Assyrian invasion in 701 B.C. He asserted the supremacy of Yahweh, the God of Israel, emphasising his moral standards and divine holiness. According to tradition he was martyred. See **C4.3** below.

**3e.1**    A large hawk (14thC)

**3e.2**    Part of a dragon (14thC)

**3e.3**    A fine dragon (14thC)

## BORDERS OF THE MAIN LIGHTS

There are three distinct border types. Everything of note in the borders is listed within the descriptions of each panel.

Type A.
The borders of the three centre panels are alternate fleur-de-lis and rosettes set against pieces of plain ruby. (14thC) – but some of these are modern copies. In white glass touched with yellow stain. Each fleur-de-lis and rose, both emblems of the Virgin Mary, is in a diamond shaped frame. An almost identical design can be seen in the borders of the panels in the east window of the south aisle at Stanford -on-Avon. Fleur-de-lis, as at Merevale, can also be seen at Wroxall (Warwickshire), Bushby (Staffordshire), at North Luffenham (Rutland), and at Thornton (Leicestershire).

Type B.
In the borders of all the other panels  there are thirty-four pieces of glass, too numerous to list, consisting of pieces of a vertical stem with off-springing oak leaves and acorns interspersed with thirteen grotesque winged dragons, or parts of dragons. These latter are all listed. (14thC)

The vertical stem is white, the dragons each perch on a small trefoil leaf, their necks are twisted around the stem, and they bite themselves.  Mostly they bite their feathered wings but in the borders of **2e** and **3a** they seem to bite their tails. The stem and dragons are white glass touched with yellow stain. The oak leaves are either green and leaded independently of the stem, or are white touched yellow stain and on the same piece of glass as the stem.

Type C.
There are two hawks in profile facing left. In white glass , their beaks and claws are in yellow stain.(14C) A general comparison can be made between the birds in the glass at Stanford-on-Avon, birds in the Bestiary section of the Queen Mary's Psalter, birds in the mural decoration of the Longthorpe Tower, near Peterborough, and the birds inhabiting the vine at Ludlow and at Merevale. All these date from 1330-1340.

The remaining part of the borders are filled  with very many other fragments of medieval glass. It would seem that many of these are related to the four hundred and fifty-three pieces found in a box labelled 'Box of Glass from Merevale Church' which was located in the muniments room at Merevale Hall in 1991 (see note following details of window **n111**). Three hundred and twenty of these have been photographed by the author, and also by the R.C.H.M.E. for their national archives. A large number  of the pieces would appear to have come out of widows **n11** and **nV** presumably when the Victorian memorial windows were inserted. Some of the glass also came from **n111** and **n1V**, and from elsewhere in the church. (See Appendix E)

## Note on animals, birds and dragons

For the people of the Middle Ages the origin of the animals was explained in Genesis and was rooted, like all else, in God's work. They were fascinated not only by the animals and birds that they could see, but also by a whole other world of imaginary, exotic, and mythological beasts. The design of these are echoed in the manuscripts, sculpture and stained glass of the period as will be shown below. These medieval images are especially engaging, for they are able to charm, amuse, and instruct, and all at the same time. In the medieval glass of the Merevale Jesse there are no less than twenty-four creatures i.e. thirteen winged dragons biting themselves, two hawks, four other birds, two squirrels sitting on their hind legs eating nuts, two owls and a small monkey.

It will be seen that the birds and the pieces of vine stem on which they perch are painted on the same piece of glass. The other animals are leaded independently of the stem.

It could well be mentioned here that there is a tendency in Gothic art to a certain excessiveness, a habit of breaking the rules, overstepping the mark and inventing curious images irrelevant or somehow superfluous to the theological doctrine. This is particularly evident in marginal drawings. The French call them *drôlieres* and Andrew Graham-Dixon refers to the idea as *baboonery*.[1]  Apart perhaps from the animals in the glass, there are also associated with Merevale the marginal drawings in the Rydeware Cartulary which is said to have been written by the monks in the scriptorium of the Abbey (see Appendix F).[2] These consist of fantastic dogs and rabbits returning from the hunt. The rabbits are blowing trumpets to announce their killing of a pig, and another pig, sitting astride a dog is helping to carry a dead pheasant. Another rabbit, standing on its hind legs, has a long-bow. This development reached its apogee in the fourteenth century in the often riotous treatment of many East Anglian books, such as the Gorleston and Ormesby psalters.[3]

It should be remembered that no less an authority than St Bernard of Clairvaux denounced the unseemly exuberance in early twelfth-century Cluniac art. His vitriolic condemnation was a protest both against the distractive influence and the extravagance of this type of ornament. This protest was echoed by  Adam, a Cistercian monk of Dore Abbey, in the early thirteenth century who was 'struck with grief that in the sanctuary of God there should be foolish pictures of monkeys and monstrosities'. This was all to no avail as the ornamental motifs both in religious manuscripts, sculpture  and stained glass became common from the early Middle Ages. Just as the exclusive domain of the Church included close involvement with the secular affairs, so religious art incorporated profane elements, often giving them symbolic overtones.


The iconography of dragons.

The dragon/serpent/snake was the creature most used in medieval art as a symbol of sin/evil/heresy.  In biting themselves the dragons are trying to gain redemption. (the Greek word *drakon* meant large serpent as well as dragon and the Latin *draco* means dragon or snake. Romans sometimes   kept   non-poisonous   snakes as household pets, which were called *dracunculi*).  In the Old Testament the dragon is the source of death and sin, a conception which was adopted in the New Testament and so passed into the Christian mythology of the Middle Ages. The dragon was seen as representing the devil and all his works. In Genesis the snake was the creature selected to tempt Adam and Eve to disobey God's commandment. It is sometimes depicted as a devil-headed dragon.  The establishment of the Order of the Vanquished Dragon in 1418 by the Holy Roman Emperor Sigismund, who was also King of Bohemia, celebrated the victory of orthodoxy over the Bohemian Reformer and heretic Jan Hus. The image of the conquered dragon was used as  the symbol of heresy overcome. The life stories of numerous saints include the defeat of a dragon to symbolise the triumph of good over evil, i.e. SS George, Juliana, Michael (Rev. xii.9 'that old serpent called the Devil, and Satan'), Martha, and Silvester, and also four who are represented in this church. In the north aisle there is St Margaret (**2e** in **n1V**) and St John (**2f** in **n111**)  and, in the south aisle, the obscure St. Armel (**3** in **s1V**). A dragon was also one of the attributes of St Bernard of Clairvaux, the founder of the Cistercian Order, whose armorial bearings are **A2** in **1**..

Examples in twelfth-century Romanesque sculpture of dragons biting themselves in a very similar manner to those at Merevale can be seen in a capital at the Cathedral of Santiago de Compostela in Spain, biting their legs, and in a capital at Saint-Pierre, Aulnay, in France, biting their tails. In both places the dragons also have wings, as do those at Merevale. There are also two winged dragons in a late twelfth-century Flemish Book of Hours which is in the Walters Art Gallery in Baltimore, U.S.A. One is biting its neck and the other its right leg.[4] They are again very similar to the Merevale dragons.

The representation of a dragon or serpent biting its own tail is a urboros, a tail-devourer. However it more usually appears in northern European art in the form of a circle and is used to symbolise completion and perfection.

1    Graham-Dixon 1996, p 28.
2    Wrottesley  1895.
3    Crewe 1987, p 52.
4    Randall 1966, p 68.

## THE TRACERY LIGHTS

**A1** A large ruby flower. (14thC)

**A1.1** Head of a man facing three-quarters right. Technique as **C1.5** The head has been reversed. (14thC)

**A1.2** Pieces of white foliage as **C7**. (14thC)

**A2** A Shield
Argent a band chequy over all a pastoral staff erect. On a white ground powered rosettes in yellow stain. In situ. (15thC)

The shield is painted in black lines on white glass, no tincture. An adaption of the arms of the Cistercian Order. (St Bernard ?)

**A3** A Shield
Vair or and gules. FERRERS. Earl Robert de Ferrers founded Merevale Abbey in 1148; he gave to it 'all my Forest of Arden'. This is also the coat of arms of the Abbey. See **A8**.

On a white ground powdered with continuous circles each enclosing a rosette in yellow stain; in a plain yellow stain border. In situ. (15thC)

**A4** Head of a king, crowned, facing three-quarters left. (15thC)

**A4.1** Pieces of white foliage. (14thC)

**A4.2** Two pieces of stiff leaf foliage design on a cross-hatched ground. Very decayed. (13thC)

**A5** St Gabriel, the Angel of the Annunciation
Stands full length facing three-quarters right, in his left hand a scroll inscribed, in black letter:

AVE MARI

Wears a white tunic powdered with foliage sprays, in yellow stain. The head is missing. The scroll is incomplete, part of the remaining words have scaled off. (15thC.)

**A6** The Virgin of the Annunciation
Stands full length facing three-quarters left, holding a scroll inscribed, in black letter:-

DNI

an abbreviation of DOMINI, (the Lord), in her right hand.

The Virgin's dress is identical with that of the Angel, as **A5** above. Painted in black lines on white glass, the hair and dress touched yellow stain. (15thC)

**A7**  Piece of a vine stem, and a leaf. (14thC)

**A7.1**  Pieces of a border design from a tracery light. (14thC)

**A7.2**  Head of a man facing three-quarters right. (14thC)

**A7.3**  Three pieces of stiff-leaf foliage on  a cross-hatched ground. Very decayed. (14thC)

**A8**  A Shield
Argent a crozier erect or between a crescent or and a star or. Ground and border identical with **A2** above. In situ. The shield is incomplete, the head of the crozier is missing. (15thC)
   This shield is of the seal of the Abbey of Merevale. The thirteenth-century seal has the Virgin and Child under a canopy, with a hand holding a crozier and a star on the right. The armorial bearings of Cistercian Abbeys were those of their Founders. See **A3**.

**A9**  A Shield
Gules three roach naiant in pale argent, a canting device.  Ground and border identical with **A3** above. In situ. (de la Roche).  (15thC)

ELLEN DE LA ROCHE married EDMUND FERRERS of Chartley (c. 1386-1435). The window is connected with the Ferrers family, as **B5.1**, also the fragments detailed in **C1** and **C2.1** which contain quarries with their horseshoe device.

**A10**  A large ruby foliage design. (14thC)

**A10.1**Head of a man facing three-quarters left. The hem of his tunic is patterned. (14thC)

**B1**  Head of a man facing three-quarters right wearing a ruby coloured cap. This head has been reversed.   (14thC)

**B1.1**  Pieces of  white foliage design, from tracery lights as **C7** below. (14thC)

**B2**  White quarries as **B5**  below. (15thC)
At the top there is a buttercup flower with petals yellow stained.

**B3**    Head of a man facing three-quarters right. This head has been reversed. (14thC)

**B3.1**    Pieces of white foliage design from tracery lights.

**B3.2**    At the very top of the light is a women, shown half length, and facing three-quarters left. To the right of the figure is written '60'. White glass (16thC)

**B4**    Head of a man facing three-quarters left. (14thC)

**B4.1**    Pieces of white foliage design, from tracery lights. (14thC)

**B5**    Flower with petals yellow stained. The flowers at the bottom of the light are of a very delicate and stylised design.

**B5.1**    White quarries, each bearing a horseshoe – the Ferrers' device – in yellow stain. (15thC)

**B6**    Head of a King, crowned, facing three-quarters left. (14thC)

**B6.1**    Pieces of white foliage design.


<u>A Panel of Fragments</u>
**C1**    A horseshoe – the Ferrers' device – in yellow stain. A typical heraldic play on words, known as canting, (Fers de cheval : horse shoes). Unless otherwise blazoned, the armorial horseshoe has its points downwards.

**C1.1**    A French wife's hood, bound, painted in black lines. (15th.C, not earlier than 1475)
    This is a badge of the Deveraux family. It was first used by Sir Walter Deveraux (c.1432-1485), of Weobley, Herefordshire, 7th Baron Ferrers of Chartley. He married Anne, daughter and heir of Sir William de Ferrers of Chartley. He was summoned to Parliament as Lord Ferrers from 1461 onwards and he was on Edward IV's expedition to France in July 1475. The badge was worn by the contingent of men-at-arms and 200 archers taken to France by Lord Ferrers, and adopted by him afterwards.[1]  The badge was described as a 'ffrench wyfis hood boundyn'. In view of the animosity between France and England in these closing phases of the Hundred Years War, the description was presumably a mockingly derogatory one, implying a hood of such unfashionable cut that only a peasant woman would have worn it.[2] After a lifetime of active support for the Yorkist cause and dynasty,

Lord Ferrers was killed at the Battle of Bosworth in 1485. His grandson Sir Walter Deveraux, to whom the Abbey was granted after the Dissolution, displayed both family badges on his standard – the Ferrers's horseshoe and the Deveraux hood. In the illustration of the standard, below, there is also the Deveraux white greyhound, gorged, ie with a crown round its neck. A fragment of glass with a white dog's head, gorged, was found in the *Box of Glass* (see Appendix E). The two badges are also on his stall-plate as Knight of the Garter (see **3d. 1** in window **n1V**). In spite of the story of the 1475 expedition, the reason for the name of the hood remains a mystery. The first Sir Walter's grandmother was a Roche (see **A.9** above) and one meaning of *rochet* in Old French is a 'hood'. Perhaps it is another canting name. By 'bound' is meant the cord tied round it, not unlike a liripipe, which eventually developed into the student's hood of today. See also **A1** and **A3** in window **n1V**.

1    Barnard 1925, p 25.
2    Spencer 1990, p 104.

*Banner of Sir Walter Deveraux, 7th Baron Ferrers of Chartley, showing the Ferrers' horseshoe, the Deveraux French wife's hood and white greyhound. (From a Tudor manuscript in the College of Arms, MS 12, 115, reproduced by kind permission of the College of Arms)*

**C1.2** Fragment of an inscription, in black letter:

ORATE P AIABS

MARGRIE UXIS E (15th. C.)

This is probably part of a window, now lost, referring to Robert, Lord Ferrers of Chartley (d.1412), and his wife Margaret whose brasses are set in the chancel floor.

The translation, assuming that the abbreviations P stands for PRO, AIABS for ANIMABUS, MARGRIE for MARGARET and UXIS for UXORIS, reads – PRAY FOR THE SOULS (piece missing) OF HIS WIFE MARGARET.

It should be added that this fragment has also been associated with a window that was seen in the south aisle by William Burton in 1606 and Dugdale in 1656, and part of which is now in the National Gallery of Victoria in Australia. According to Dugdale the inscription, now missing, started with the ORATE PR ANIMABUS. The window was donated by John Handewell, of Coventry (d. 1365). Because of the late date of this fragment the derivation seems unlikely, also his wife's name was Alice, not Margaret. See Note on Lost Glass which ends the description of Window **s.11**.

**C1.3** Fragment of a gable, in yellow stain, inscribed in black letter:

PARATE VIAM DNI (15thC)

This is possibly a fragment from a quotation from Isaiah (xl.3) VOX CLAMANTIS IN DEFERRO: PARATE VIAM DOMINI, – A VOICE CRYING IN THE WILDERNESS: PREPARE THE WAY OF THE LORD -.

**C1.4** As **C1**

**C1.5** Head of a man facing three-quarters left, in white glass.

**C1.6** A bourchier knot, made up of two horseshoe shapes of rope intertwined. It is a 'granny' knot. Painted in black lines on white glass.

A badge of the Bourchier family. These included Henry Bourchier, 1st Earl of Essex, Treasurer of England, married Isobel, aunt of Edward 1V, (d.1483), and Cardinal Thomas Bouchier (1404-?-1486), Lord Chancellor, Archbishop of Canterbury, crowned Edward 1V(1461) and Richard 111(1483). Raised troops for the restoration to the throne of Edward 1V in 1471.

**C1.7** Head of a child with long hair, facing right.

**C1.8** A French wife's hood, bound, as **C1.1** above. Painted in black lines. (15th.C, not earlier than 1475)

**C1.9** Head of a youth, in profile facing left, in white glass, the hair in yellow stain. (15thC)

**C1.10** Section of a border of a roundel – twisted rope design. (16thC)  There is a box containing over four hundred fragments of medieval glass, some very small, in the muniments room at Merevale Hall. They were all originally in this church and were probably taken out when the Victorian memorial glass was put in. They have been photographed and recorded by the R.C.H.M.E. Amongst them  is a 16th C Flemish roundel of Jonah being thrown to the whale, the border of which is identical to **C4.10**, similar to **C5.7**.

**C1.11** A large piece of white glass patterned with a conventionalised pomegranate design in yellow stain. (15th – 16th C.)

**C1.12** A seagull-type bird in yellow stain, with yellow beak and outstretched wings; a crest, a device borne on the helm of an armorial coat of arms. This from the fact the bird is standing on a wreath, or torse – always with six twists, as here – derived from the coloured pieces of fabric which hid the join of the crest to the helm. (15th C ?)

## A Panel of Fragments

**C2** A small head of Christ facing three-quarters right, in white glass, the head and beard in yellow stain, the nimbus white, the cross in yellow stain. (14thC)

**C2.1** A French wife's hood, bound, as **C1.1** (15th C, not earlier than 1475)

**C2.2** Incomplete figure of Christ in Majesty (?). The torso only, facing three-quarters left, the right hand raised in benediction holding an open book on his knees, in white glass. (15thC)

**C2.3** The Ferrers' horseshoe device, as **C1.**

**C2.4** A small bearded head facing three-quarters right, in white glass, the hair is in yellow stain, – and nimbed? (14thC)

**C2.5** A French wife's hood, bound, as **C1.1.** (15th C, not earlier than 1475)

**C2.6**  A small head of a Saint facing three-quarters left, in white glass, the hair and beard in yellow stain, the nimbus white. (14thC)

**C2.7**  Part of the border of a Flemish roundel, as **C1.10** (16thC)

**C2.8**  A piece of glass from a tracery light, a sun rayon in yellow stain against a hatched ground, in a plain border, in yellow stain. (15thC)

**D1**  Scraps of white foliage work, part of a white tympanum enclosing a spray of foliage. A large rosette, in yellow. (14thC)

**D2**  Scraps of white foliage, a large green rosette. (14thC)

**E1**  Scraps of white foliage. Two white tympanum pieces each enclosing a spray of white foliage. (14thC)

**E2**  Fragments of a foliage design, from a tracery light. White serrated leaves against a black background in a border patterned with a repeated design of circles separated one from the other by two dots, in yellow stain. (14thC)

**F1**  Fragments of a white foliage design from a tracery light. (14thC)

**F1.1**  Head of a king, crowned, facing three-quarters left. (14thC)

**F1.2**  As **F1.1**

**F2**  Head of a King, crowned, facing three-quarters left. Painted in black lines on white glass, the hair and beard in yellow stain, slight matt staining around the eyes; the crown in yellow stain  is leaded separately (14thC)

# Window n11

h. 3.60 m. – w. 1.76 m.

This window is of the late nineteenth century, and is by Clayton and Bell. See Appendix C – *Victorian Glass Manufacturers.*

**1a**    A foliage design

**1b**    The inscription reads: **"This window was erected in 1875 by STEPHEN and MARY ELLEN SCOTT to the Memory of ROBERT JENNINGS, of Atherstone, Architect, who died 7th.March, 1874".**

**1c**    As **1a**

**2a**    A sun rayon design.

**2a.1**  As **1a**

**2b**    King Solomon holding in his left hand the Temple at Jerusalem, of which he was the chief architect. In his right hand he holds a sceptre. The point is not lost that this is a memorial window to an architect.

It had been thought that the canopies were modern design copies of the medieval canopies in **n111** and **n1V.** However Sarah Brown, of the R.C.H.M.E., has pointed out that Clayton and Bell were doing work at All Souls College Chapel, Oxford, in the 1870s and the design may also have been influenced by the design of the canopies there.

**2c**    As **2a**

**2c.1**  As **1a**

**A3** and **A4**    Angels singing **ALLELULIA.**

**C1** and **C2**    Angels singing **ALLELULIA.**

## Window n111.

h. 3.60 m. – w. 1.76 m.

This window and **n1V** were probably glazed between 1520 – 1530. See <u>Note on dating</u> at the end of this window.

**2a**    Fragments of a canopy, almost intact, on a blue ground.

**2b**    Canopy of fragmented glass, on a ruby ground. Below, part of a panel depicting the Assumption of the Virgin (?), surrounded by four rather rustic angels with crosses on their heads. The iconoclasts of the Reformation would often mutilate the head of a figure of Christ or the Virgin rather than  the whole panel.

In the east window of the Church of Saints Peter and Paul, East Harling, Norfolk, there is a panel depicting the Assumption of the Blessed Virgin. (15thC)  The Virgin is seen ascending to Heaven attended by angels, a crown above her head. Here at Merevale there are fragments of a very similar panel. The crosses on the angels' heads in both windows, are almost identical. The crown above the Virgin's head is possibly amongst the fragments in **1a** in **n1V.** Over the centuries there has been much rearrangement of the glass. The Virgin's head and aureole, found in the box of glass at Merevale Hall (see *Appendix E*) are of a very similar date and style, but they do not belong to this panel. One reason for this is that the Virgin found in the box of glass has a hand, and there are already two hands in **1a** in **n111.**

**2c**    Very similar to **2a.**

The following six lights contain the figures of six Apostles, in yellow stain.

**A1**    St Thomas surnamed Didymus, i.e. the twin. Little is known about him apart from his unbelief and subsequent profession of faith in Christ's resurrection. (John xx:24 etc) In art he is shown as an elderly man holding a lance or spear, as here.

**A2**    St James the Greater. The son of Zebedee and Salome and brother of St John the Evangelist. He was the first of the Apostles to be martyred (Acts xii:2), under King Herod Agrippa. A ninth-century legend makes him the military apostle of Spain. His relics are preserved in the Cathedral at Santiago de Compostella. The legend grew, under Cluniac influence, and spread throughout Western Europe, so that Compostela became, after Jerusalem and Rome, the most famous place of pilgrimage in Christendom in the Middle

Ages. St James is the patron saint of Spain. Santiago is Spanish for St James, and Compostella is a corruption of *Giacomo-postolo* (James the Apostle). He is depicted as elderly and bearded, with a hat with a scallop shell on it, or with shell or shells about him. He is dressed as a pilgrim with a wallet (a scrip), and his 'staff of faith'. He is identified here by the scallop shell on his cloak. There is a fragment of a tiled floor.

> 'Give me my scallop shell of quiet,
> My staff of faith to walk upon,
> My scrip of Joy, Immortal diet,
> My bottle of salvation:
> My Gown of Glory, hopes true gage,
> And thus I'll take my pilgrimage'.
>           Sir Walter Raleigh.

(The St James's scallop is the great scallop – *Pectens maximus* - known locally as *Vieira*, and the basis of Coquille St Jacques. This is a cookery note.)

**A3**   St Philip, Apostle. Appears infrequently in the Gospels. He is associated with the Feeding of the Five Thousand (John vi:5), hence the loaves in his left hand – his usual attribute. After the Ascension he is believed to have preached in Asia Minor, and to have been martyred at Hierapolis in Phrygia. He is standing on a tiled floor.

**A4**   St Bartholomew, Apostle. One of the disciples of whom little is known. The tradition is that he travelled east as far as India. While preaching in Armenia he was seized by heathens, flayed alive and crucified. Thus his invariable attribute is a large knife of peculiar shape, which he holds here in his left hand. He stands on a tiled floor.

**A5**   St Peter. Holding two keys, and with an open book. The culminating episode narrated of him in the Gospel is that of his confession of Christ as the Son of God (Matthew xvi:15-19), to which Christ answered with the solemn promise: "You are Peter and upon this rock I will build my church....and I will give you the keys of the kingdom of Heaven". There is a single fragment of a tiled floor.

**A6**   St John. There are one hundred and seventy-eight saints called John according to the Roman Church. This is the Apostle and Evangelist. He was a brother of St James the Greater, and a fisherman. He became 'the Disciple whom Jesus loved', whom Our Lord, dying on the Cross, made the guardian of His mother. He is seen, as is usual in Christian art, as a young man, and holding a goblet in which there is a little dragon. This alludes to the occasion when, according to legend, the Emperor Domitian ordered him to drink a cup of poisoned wine. When John took up the cup to obey, the poison departed in the form of a snake or dragon.

**C1**   This tracery light has not been seen since 1960. In 1947 the *Victoria County History* described it as a 'red roundel (17th century and foreign) showing a king (Pharaoh?[1]) seated in a golden canopied chariot drawn by four horses, troops of pikeman one side and archers on the other, and spearman behind. Fragments about it included a smaller roundel with a man's head, brown feathers of a wing, some letters 'Raad Burg', etc.'

In 1960 Dr Newton stated that the apex of the window contained a 14th C. roundel. It showed a bust length figure of a youth facing three-quarters left, bareheaded, wearing a tunic with a chaperon over his shoulders. Either side of the figure was a spray of two oak leaves and acorns.

A Walpole Society publication of 1930 – *The Glass Paintings of Coventry and its Neighbourhood* by Bernard Rackham, (Walpole Society, Vol X1X, JJJ. 3. 56., British Museum) confirms both the 'chariot' of the V.C.H. and the 'youth's head' of Newton by description and by a photograph. As late as 1966 Pevsner states that 'in a north aisle window there is a small 14th C head'.

It would seem likely that the 'king seated in a golden chariot' was a Flemish roundel of the 16th C. as was  **C1** in **n1V.** Both lights are blocked up by pieces of wood. It should be noted that the pieces of wood on the outside of the church are perhaps not the same as those inside. It may be possible that both panels of glass are still there, sandwiched and protected between the wood, although presumably damaged. However without a close inspection, with a ladder, it is impossible to be certain, either way.  In the box of fragments of medieval glass, once in the church and  now at Merevale Hall, there is a complete Flemish roundel of Jonah being thrown to the whale. The border to it is complete and is identical to **C4.10** in **1** and **C5.7** in **1.** Although there is a problem with the  mullions  in **n11** and **nV,** it is possible that there were Flemish roundels in the top lights of all four of the north aisle windows which were all glazed 1520 – 1530.

### Note on Dating

The north aisle seems to have been rebuilt in the early sixteenth century. The tracery light glazing in  **n111** and **n1V** is of a similar character, but there are some differences between the canopies of the main lights. Nonetheless, the tracery designs of the windows are uniform, which suggests that the rebuilding and glazing were carried out in one operation. This is supported by antiquarian evidence of lost glass. William Burton visited Merevale in 1606 and again in 1629. Both he and Dugdale (prior to 1656) recorded in the north aisle windows the arms of the See of Bangor impaling **'On a Chevron between three doves and in chief three gilly flowers with three amulets'** surrounded by a mitre and with this inscription below:

**Dn̄s Tho: Skevēton ep̄us de Bangagēsis hanc fenestr̄a fieri fecit.**
**Thomas consecratus 1509 1:H:8 obiit.** (piece of page missing)
**1533:25:h:8.B**

Thomas Skevington was the son of John and Margaret Pace, and was probably born in Skeffington in Leicestershire. His mother was the daughter and heiress of William Cobley. He was a monk at Merevale, and by 1509 was appointed Abbot of Beaulieu in Hampshire. In the same year he became Bishop of Bangor and he held both posts until his death. Skevington's body was buried at Beaulieu and his heart at Bangor. There are floor tiles with his coat of arms at Beaulieu. To his old home at Merevale he gave this window as his memorial. At the Church of St Thomas à Becket in Skeffington there was a window with the inscription 'Orate pro Thomas Pace.Quondam Episcopo Bangor'.[2]

Although the antiquarian sources do not give the exact location of this window, it can be assumed with confidence it was one of those in the north aisle. It must have been near that commemorating John Handewell, a former reeve of Coventry, and his wife, which contained this inscription:

> **Orate pro animabus Johis Handewell quandam pretoris Coventrie**
> **et Alice uxoris eius, qui isturm fenestram unacum opere amato ubi**
> **tumulatur tumulo de alabasto, in partibus borealibus et sumptibus**
> **suis proprius fieri fecit, quorum animabus miseretur deus amen.**
> (Pray for the soul of John Handewell, formerly chief magistrate of
> Coventry, and Alice his wife, who caused this window to be made as
> an act of love in the place where he is buried, together with a tomb of
> alabster, on the north side, and entirely at his own expense. On whose
> souls, my Lord, have mercy. Amen)

See also **C4.2** in **1** and <u>Note on lost glass</u> which concludes **s11**.

On his tomb, now also missing, was a largely illegible inscription which ended with the date 1524. There are four windows in the north aisle and the Skevington and Handewell inscriptions may have come from the two that retain some of their glazing. They at least provide evidence that the north aisle windows were glazed around 1520 – 1530.[3]

1   Harris 1937, p 129.
2   Newton 1961, p 928.
3   Norton 1986, p 222-223.

## Window n1V

h.3.60 m. – w. 1.76 m.

This window and **n111** were probably glazed around 1520 – 1530. See <u>Note on dating</u> that follows the description of **n111**.

**3a**    A canopy made of fragments, but there are parts of figures including St John the Baptist. In the bottom half is his emblem – the Lamb of God – holding a reed cross with a banner on it, slipped in, as it were, in a curious manner between the leaves of a half open book.

**3b**    This panel is made up of fragments. In the bottom half is a crown with a jewelled circlet.

**3c**    <u>A Shield</u>
Vair or, and gules. FERRERS. Similar to **A3** in **1**, very decayed. (14thC)

**3c.1**    The head of what looks like a mouse (ferret/Ferrer?). Decayed. (14thC) .

**3c.2**    The guard, grip, and pommel of a sword. Possibly a fragment from a coat of arms recorded by Dugdale ( no 7, p.783, 1656 edition), but now unidentified.

**A1**    A panel of fragments.

**A2**    The figure of the risen Christ with St Mary Magdelene, known as a 'Noli me tangere'. This comes from John xvii. 20 – Jesus said to her (Mary Magdelene) "Touch me not, for I have not yet ascended to my Father".
   Note that the risen Christ is partly hidden from the kneeling Magdelene by an olive tree, with lopped branches, treated in a highly formalised manner. The drawing here, as in the rest of these panels, seems crude.

**A3**    St Gabriel, the Angel of Annunciation.
The treatment of the wings is very curious. They seem to be held together with a cord through eyelets, which must be similar to something, somewhere.

**A4**    A figure of the Virgin kneeling  before a desk with an open book. In the angular folds of the draperies, and the placing of the Virgin beneath a square tester with rolled up curtains, there is perhaps a recognisable Flemish influence.
   The above two lights combine to form the subject of the Annunciation, as are **A5** in **1** and **A6** in **1,** appropriate enough in a church dedicated to Our Lady.

**A4.1** A fragment of a buckle  and the letters '**H O N**'. This is part of the Garter ('Honi soit qui mal y pense' – motto of the Order of the Garter) which encircled the Devereaux quartering Ferrers coat of arms, illustrated and recorded by Dugdale as being in a window in the church prior to 1656.  This could be part of the armorial bearings of Sir  Walter Devereaux, 1st Earl of Essex, who was made Knight of the Garter in 1572, or his son, Robert Devereaux who was knighted in 1588. Robert Devereaux, second earl of Essex was a favourite of Queen Elizabeth. He was sent to Tower and beheaded when he fell from grace with his Royal Mistress. He remarked, in her presence, that 'her mind was as crooked as her carcase.' (see Chapter 2 – *The Succession of Owners of Merevale Estate.)*

In the box of glass found at Merevale Hall (see Appendix E) there is a fragment with a white greyhound's head, gorged, with a coronet, which is a supporter on the Devereaux coat-of-arms, obviously originally attached to this piece. See the illustration of the Deveraux standard following **C1.1** in window **1**.

In the Burrell Collection, in Glasgow, there is an similar piece of glass of the arms of Sir Henry Fitzhugh (d. 1424), surrounded by the garter.

**A5** St Margaret with a cross-tipped spear and a dragon. She is said to have been a maiden of Antioch in Pisidia, and martyred under Diocletian. Legends about her include the story of the dragon which swallowed her before she was beheaded. Nevertheless she is one of the most popular of the maiden-martyr saints and her cult is very ancient. In art she is shown trampling or standing on a dragon, as here, and piercing it with a spear. The cult was suppressed by the Roman Church in 1969.

**A6** St Anne teaching the Virgin to read. The Gospels do not mention the names of the Virgin's parents. Tradition gives his mother as Anne. The St Anne cult appears in the sixth century in Eastern liturgies and in the eighth in the West but it did not become general until the end of the fourteenth century. St Anne is usually represented as teaching her daughter to read the Bible, or greeting her husband St Joachim at the Golden Gate.

**B1** Horseshoes – the Ferrers device – and a French wife's hood, bound, see **C1** in **1** and **C1.1** in **1**. (15thC).

**B2** As **B1** above.

**C1** This tracery light has been removed since 1947, when the *Victoria County History* described it as 'a roundel depicting the Ascension'. Mary Dormer Harris described it in 1937 and wrote 'You may see the impression of Christ's feet on the mountain top.'[1]  But see note on **A1** in **n11**.

---

[1]   Harris 1937, p 129.

## Window nV.

### h. 3.60m. – w. 1.76m.

This window is of the late nineteenth century, and is by Burlison and Grylls. See Appendix C – *Victorian Glass Manufacturers*.

The four Evangelists are shown symbolically in this window. Ezekial i:10 first mentions the four living creatures, and this was taken up by St John the Divine in Revelation iv:7. The Fathers of the Church, especially St Jerome, interpreted them as symbolic personifications of the four Gospel-makers.

**1a**  A winged lion is St Mark's invariable attribution, presumably because his Gospel emphasises the royal dignity of Christ, Lion of Judah. It is with the relevant description.

**1b**  The inscription reads **'To the glory of God, and in loving memory of WILLIAM EDWARD MINION, born April 26th 1824, died January 18th 1879'.**

William Edward Minion was a farmer who lived at Abbey Farm. He was a member of an Atherstone family who were warfingers, millers, and corn merchants for over a hundred years. They owned Minion's Wharf and the mill in Coleshill Road near the Coventry Canal. He was elected Churchwarden at Merevale in 1850.

**1c**  St John is the eagle, the messenger of the word of God, soaring above the world. With the inscription of his name.

**2a**  St Matthew is shown as a man, or an angel, which is his main emblem. Because he first recorded the human ancestry of Christ he is sometimes shown as holding a pen and inkwell, etc. Here he is holding a scroll with his name on it.

**2b**  In this main light Jesus is depicted as the sower, as in Mark iv : 3-8. The inscription reads **"Behold the sower went forth to sow".** The point is not lost that this is a memorial window to a miller and a corn merchant.

**2c**  The winged ox, or calf, representing St Luke. In his Gospel he emphasised the priesthood of Christ, and the ox is a symbol of sacrifice.

The following six tracery lights contain angels displaying the instruments, or symbols, of the Passion.

**A1**   After the Crucifixion the soldiers cast lots for Christ's cloak which was 'without seam, woven, from the top throughout'.

**A2**   When Pilate had reluctantly agreed to the demands of the mob and had released Barabbas, he delivered Jesus to the soldiers to be flogged.

**A3**   Clubs usually refer to the betrayal of Christ, as in Mark xiv:43. The pillar is that to which Christ was bound in order to be whipped.

**A4**   Three nails and the Crown of Thorns. Early crucifixes show four nails, piercing each of the hands and feet of Christ. On most crucifixes there are only three, both feet being pierced by one nail. The number three was preferred perhaps because of the symbolic reference to the Trinity.

**A5**   Pincers are generally shown with the hammer which was used for driving in the nails; possibly the nails were held by the pincer. Joseph of Arimathea is sometimes depicted in scenes pulling out the nails at the taking down of Jesus from the Cross.

**A6**   The spear because it was used to pierce the side of Christ, and the sponge because of the story in Matthew xxvii:48, are also emblems of the Crucifixion.

**C1**   i̅h̅s̅  This monogram was first found on the tombs of early Christians in the Roman catacombs. The sign represented the first three letters of the name of Jesus in Greek. The omission of the other letters is shown by the bar, which is a mark of abbreviation.

**C2**   x̅p̅s̅  This more unusual monogram represents the first, second, and the last letters of the name of Christ in Greek. The sign of the bar is again used.

## Window s11

h. 4.80 m. w. 1.96 m.

This window was inserted in 1885, and is by Burlison and Grylls. Although similar in date to **nV** it shows their late-medieval Germanic style. (See Appendix C – *Victorian Glass Manufacturers*)

**1a**   **W.S.D**.

**1b**   <u>A Shield</u>
Quarterly 1 and 4 argent a cross moline gules charged with a King of Arms' coronet or, in the first quarter a torteau. DUGDALE: 2 and 3 barry of ten argent and azure a lion rampant gules STRATFORD impaling. Gules the base barry wavy argent and azure issuing therefrom a demi horse rampant argent hoofed and maned or. TREVELYAN.

**1b.1**   The inscription reads: **"To the Glory of God this window is placed in memory of WILLIAM STRATFORD DUGDALE Esq., who died May 9th. 1882, by his tenantry."**
For biographical details of William Stratford Dugdale see under 'The Dugdale Family' in Chapter 2 – *The Succession of Owners of the Merevale Estate*. His wife, Alice Dugdale, is commemorated by the plaque in the north-east corner of the family pew where she used to sit. (see memorial **M28**)

**1c**   as **2a.**

**2a**   St Paul's miraculous release from prison in Phillippi.(Acts xvi:26-30). The inscription reads: **"For he hath broken the gates of brass, and cut the bars of iron in sunder"**. (Psalms cvii:16)

**2b**   Joseph being lifted up out of the pit before being sold to the Ishmaelites – with the pieces of silver being exchanged, and his coat of many colours. (Genesis xxxvi:28). The inscription reads **"Out of the depth have I cried unto thee O Lord"**. (Psalms cxxx:1).

**2c**   The Fiery Furnace. The inscription reads: **"They shall not thirst any more, neither shall any heat light on them, & God shall wipe away all tears from their eyes"**. (Revelation vii:16).

**3a**   The Ascension – with the heads of other disciples in the background. The inscription reads: **"Thou hast ascended on high, thou hast led captivity captive"**. (Psalms lxviii:18)

**3b**    The Crucifixion – with Mary, the mother of Christ, St John and Mary Magdelene at the foot of the Cross. The inscription reads: **"Greater love hath no man than this, than a man lay down his life for his friends".** (John xv:13).

**3c**    Pentecost – with the Holy Spirit in the form of a dove, and the cloven tongues of fire which 'sat upon each of them' (Acts 2:4). The inscription reads: **"I will not leave you comfortless".** (John xiv:18).

**F1**    Monogram of the name of Jesus in Greek.

### Note on lost glass[1]

In 1656 Dugdale illustrated a panel in the east window of the south aisle depicting two knights in heraldic surcoats and carrying shields of arms of the Ferrers family, the founders of the Abbey. This has now disappeared, but a second panel illustrated in Dugdale, which was in one of the other south aisle windows, can be identified as now being in the National Gallery of Victoria in Melbourne, Australia. It was purchased from Thomas Grosvenor, in London, for £1,500 in 1921 by money from the Felton Bequest. Alfred Felton was the Gallery's major benefactor. The accession number is 2418.3.[2]

*Sir John de Hardreshull (d.c.1365) and his wife Margaret (National Gallery of Victoria, Melbourne)*

The panel shows a kneeling knight and his lady with their respective surcoat and gown bearing the Hardreshull arms and holding a shield with the same arms. The panel has a quatrefoil shape exactly matching the tracery of the four south aisle windows. It could not have been in **s11** because that contained the two knights, see above, or **s1V** or **sV** because these contain 'in situ' 15th-16thC and 14thC glass respectively. The Hardreshull panel must have been in **s111** and taken out when the Ward and Hughes / Dugdale memorial window was put in around 1872. It seems that it was then sold directly, or indirectly, to Grosvenor Thomas, the London dealer. The blue ground on which the figures are set has the same foliate diaper design as the roundel (?) in **s1V**.   The knight and the lady have been identified as Sir John de Hardreshull (1293/4 – c.1365) and his wife Margaret.[3] He was the last male descendant that had owned the manor of Hartshill since at least the beginning of the twelfth century. Sir John spent much of his life in the King's service and in 1329/30 was appointed commissioner of the peace in Warwickshire. His tomb is at Ashton in Northamptonshire. His alabaster effigy on a tomb-chest with panels and a ballflower frieze, in the church of St Michael, is the earliest in the county. The name is spelt Herteshull.[4] He and his wife must have been the donors of the window at Merevale in which they were depicted, and the figure style and details of the armour suggest that the glass dates from about the middle of the fourteenth century. In fourteenth-century donor glass women appear less frequently than men and rarely accompanied by their husbands.[5]

[1]   Norton 1986, p 221.
[2]   National Gallery of Victoria, personal communication 19.5.1993.
[3]   Steinberg 1939, p 438-9.
[4]   Pevsner, Northamptonshire 1973, p 94.
[5]   Marks 1993, p 11.

## Window s111

h. 3.60 m. – w. 1.87 m.

This window is of the late nineteenth century and is by Ward and Hughes, and was probably placed in the church in 1872, (see Appendix C – *Victorian Glass Manufacturers*).

**1a,1b,1c** The inscription reads: **"In Memory of WILLIAM STRATFORD DUGDALE, Died Sept. 15th.1871"**
For biographical details of William Stratford Dugdale see under 'The Dugdale Family' in Chapter 2 – *The Succession of Owners of the Merevale Estate.*

**2a**    A saint holding a chalice and a crucifix. The inscription reads: **"Faith"**.

**2a.1**   The glass is signed by the artist 'H. HUGHES, London 1872'.

**2b**    A portrayal of Our Lady, (the dedicatee of Merevale Church), holding a child and giving food to two others. The inscription reads: **"Charity"**. The child she is holding is not Jesus as there is no nimbus.

**2c**    A saint with an anchor. The inscription reads: **"Hope"**.

**F1**    An angel with the inscription **"But the greatest of these is Charity"**. (1 Corinthians xiii.13)

## Window s1V

h. 3.06m. – w.1.87m.

3a   White quarries, each bears a conventional design in black line and yellow stain. (15thC)

3b   <u>A Shield</u>
Quarterly 1 and 4 – Vair or and gules. FERRERS.
        2 and 3 – Argent a fess gules in chief three
                torteaux gules. DEVEREUX. (15thC)
One torteau is missing from the 2nd quarter.

3b.1   An incomplete grotesque head of a man, in profile facing  left. White and yellow stain.(14thC)

3c   Fragments of white quarries bearing a running tail of roses and buds, painted in black lines, the flowers in yellow stain. (15thC)

3c.1   A border piece, a lion statant or. Very decayed. (15thC)

3c.2   Two border pieces, a fleur-de-lis or
    Probably from the Montgomery coat of arms recorded by Dugdale as being in the church in 1656.

A1   A rosette with four radiating stems, each terminating in an acorn above two leaves. Painted  in black lines on white glass. Very decayed. (14thC)

A2   Two rosettes each with four radiating stems terminating in an oak leaf and acorn alternately. Painted in black lines on white glass. Very decayed. (14thC)

A3   As **A2**.

A4   As **A1**.

B2   A rosette as **B1** but with three radiating stems etc.(14thC)

D1   A circular medallion bearing a flat foliage design in ruby and blue glass, leaded separately, encircled by a stem with off-springing  oak leaves and acorns. Painted in black lines on white glass.  Very decayed. (14thC)

D2   As **D1**.

**F1**   St Armel (Armagilus, Ermel, Ermyn, Arthmael etc) died c. 552, abbot. He was a Celtic soldier-saint whose life perhaps helped compound the legend of King Arthur.[1]  His earliest known cult and life of this obscure saint date from the twelfth century. He was reputed to have been born in South Wales, was the cousin of St Samson, became a monk, and then emigrated with many kinsmen to Brittany. It was the exodus of Bretons, a Celtic race, to Brittany during the Anglo-Saxons invasions of Britain in the fifth and sixth centuries which gave it its modern name. The Cornish church of St Erme, a few miles north of Truro, is dedicated to him. With the help of King Childebert he founded two monasteries: Plouarmel and Ploermel. A fine 16th.C church at Ploermel contains eight  stained glass windows which depict scenes from his life. He was invoked to cure headaches, fever, colic, gout and rheumatism; hospitals sometimes had him as their patron. The Saint's feast day is August 16th.

From Brittany his cult spread to Normandy, Anjou and Touraine. In England it was encouraged by King Henry VII who believed that he was saved from shipwreck off the coast of Brittany by Armel's intercession. Consequently there is a statue of him in Henry VII's chapel at Westminster Abbey, and another on Cardinal Morton's tomb at Canterbury. Older examples survive on the painted reredos of Romsey Abbey[2] and an alabaster figure in St Mary Brookfield Church (London). At Stonyhurst College (Lancs) there is an alabaster panel carved in bas-relief depicting the saint which was originally in the Cistercian Abbey of Valley Crucis. To this list may now be added Merevale.

*St Armel, the face of the dragon can  be seen through the slit in the stole.*

He is generally represented in armour and a chasuble, leading a dragon with a stole around its neck. This recalls the legend that towards the end of his life he vanquished a dragon that ravaged the country and, binding it in his stole, led it to the top of a hill now called Mount-Saint-Armel and commanded it to plunge into the river below.

In **s1V** he is represented wearing a large cope fastened by a morse at the neck and open in front, disclosing a complete suit of armour. This consists of breastplate and taces, and a skirt of mail armour beneath. The legs are in plate armour and the feet encased in broad toed sabbatons. The left hand holds a crozier, and on his head is a mitre. A book is held in his right hand from which hangs his stole. Through the slit-like opening in the stole the head of the dragon can just be seen. It is very small. The armour, and the glass, is of 1500-1525. White and yellow stain. (in situ).

1    Pykitt 1986, p 3.
2    Green 1933, p 33.

## Window sV

h.3.06m .- w.1.87m.

**2a**     A monk (?) playing an organ. A roundel.

A man seated, profile facing left, painted in black lines on white glass against a ruby ground, which bears a foliage trail reserved on a black enamel ground. Very decayed, the details almost obliterated.

Fragments of quarries bear a vertical stem with off-springing trails of roses and buds, painted in black lines. (14thC)

At the date of this glass there were two types of organs. There was the Positive, those of a fixed position, and the Portative Organ. The latter were often carried in procession slung from the neck of the player, who manipulated the keys with one hand and the bellows with the other. The monk in **2a** would appear to be playing a Portative Organ.

In the Church, in the Inventory taken at the Dissolution (see Appendix G) were included 'Item. A payre of organnys, valued at £1.1.0.' Obviously there would not have been two large organs in the Church, so presumably these were Portative Organs.

**2b**     <u>Shield</u>

Argent a chevron (sable?) between eight martlets sable. Although Newton says there are eight, Marks says that there are nine and Dugdale draws ten. The tincture of the chevron is indistinct. The martlets are painted in black enamel, the same glass as the field. It is now impossible to see how many there actually are. Very decayed. (14thC)

For Apelby. Henry Apelby donated land to the Abbey in Little Sheyle.[1] Prof. Marks says that it is for Hardreshull.[2]

**2b.1**     Two border pieces. A fleur-de-lis. Deep yellow glass. Very decayed. (14thC)

**2c**     A monk (?) playing an organ. A roundel.

Identical with **2a** except for the ground which is blue. Not quite so decayed as **2a**. Quarries are the same. (14thC)

**A2** and **A3**     Two rosettes, each with four radiating stems terminating in an oak leaf and acorn alternately. Painted in black lines on white glass. (14th.)

**A1** and **A4**     A rosette with four radiating stems each terminating with an acorn above two leaves. Painted in black lines on white glass. Very decayed. (14thC)

**B1** and **B2**    A rosette as **B1** but with three radiating stems etc. (14thC)

**C1** and **C2**    A circular medallion bearing a flat foliage design in ruby and blue glass, leaded separately, encircled by a stem with off-springing oak leaves and acorns, painted in black lines on white glass. Very decayed. (14thC)

**D1**    St John the Baptist.
Full length figure facing three-quarters, holding the 'Agnus Dei' in his left hand. Blue nimbus, figure painted in black lines on white glass (?), this very decayed and is semi-opaque. The figure's thighs and torso are incomplete. Set on a ruby ground diapered with a running foliage design reserved on a black enamel ground, in a plain white border. The ground is much broken and disarrayed, pieces of green vine leaves and other alien pieces have been inserted. All very decayed. In situ. (14thC)

1    Dugdale 1656, p 782.
2    Norton 1986, p 221.

## Window sV1

h..2.2m. – w. 1.05m.

This window is late nineteenth century, and is by Wailes and Strang, (See Appendix C – *Victorian Glass Manufacturers*)

**1a**    'ALLELUIA  ALLELUIA'

**1a.1**   The inscription reads  'DOMINE  DILEXI  DECORAM DOMUS TUAE'

**1b**    'ALLELUIA  ALLELUIA'

**1b.1**   The inscription reads 'ET  LOCUM  HABITATIONIS GLORIAE  TUAE'

**2a**    The figures of Moses, with the tablets of stone, King David with his harp, and Melchizadeck with a censer. Melchizadeck was a King and Priest at Salem, who met and blessed Abraham after a battle. In Hebrews v. 6 Jesus is called a high priest 'for ever, in the line of succession to Melchizadeck.' Like Melchizadeck, Jesus is both king and priest – king of God's kingdom and a priest because he offered the sacrifice of his own life.

Considering that the window was presented by an Incumbent of the church for sixteen years, the subject matter, the priestly tradition, could not be more appropriate.

**2a.1**   The inscription reads 'WE  PRAISE THEE O GOD'

**2b**    The figures of the Blessed Virgin, with a lily, accompanied by musicians with a cymbal and a portative organ.

**2b.2**   The inscription reads 'WE ACKNOWLEDGE THEE TO BE THE LORD'

There is a brass plate immediately below the window, which is impossible to read without the use of a ladder. It says 'Presented by The Rev B. ASTLEY, Incumbent, from Michaelmas 1855 to Michaelmas 1872.'

## Window w1

h. 4.00m. – 2.22m

**1a**    An armorial fretted design repeated seven times. The central three are made up of interlacing bendlets and bendlets sinister. The outer four consist of pallets and bars, i.e. vertical and horizontal pieces, or 'square' fretting. Entirely in plain glass.

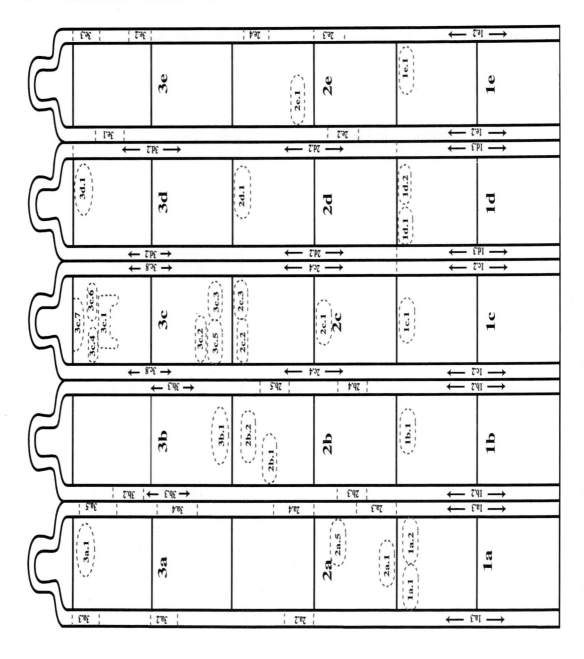

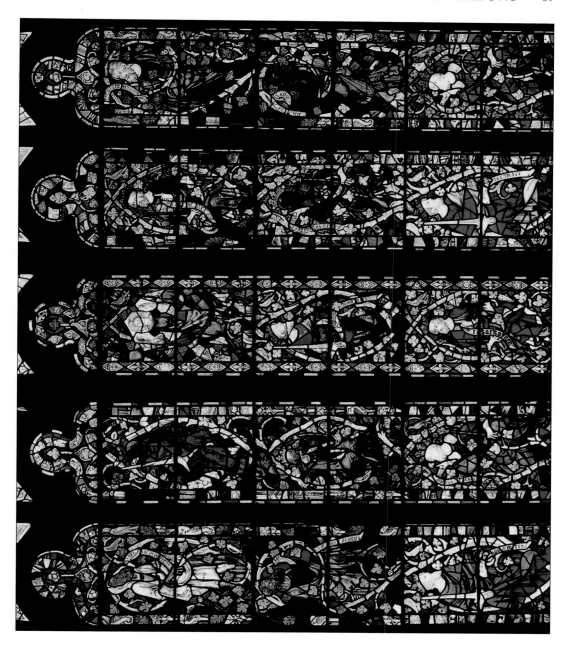

Window **1**,
*Main Lights* (RCHME,
© Crown Copyright)

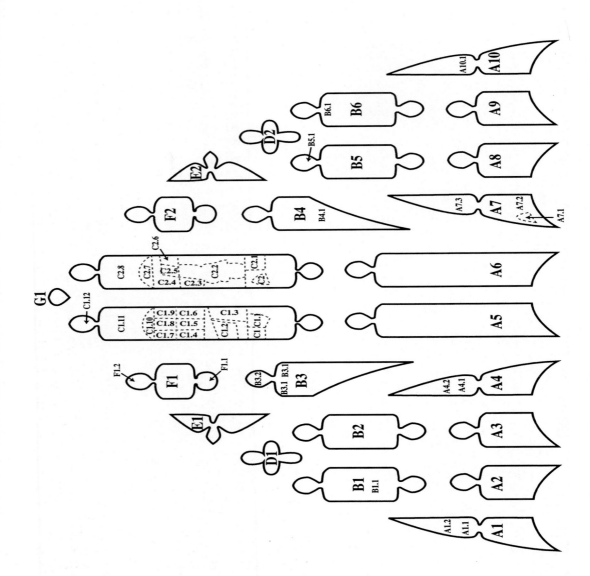

*Window* **1**, *Tracery Lights*

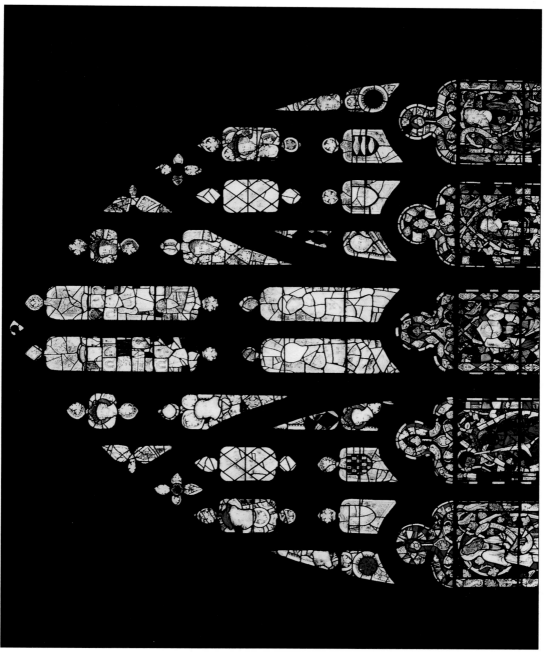

Window **1**, *Tracery Lights* (RCHME, © Crown Copyright)

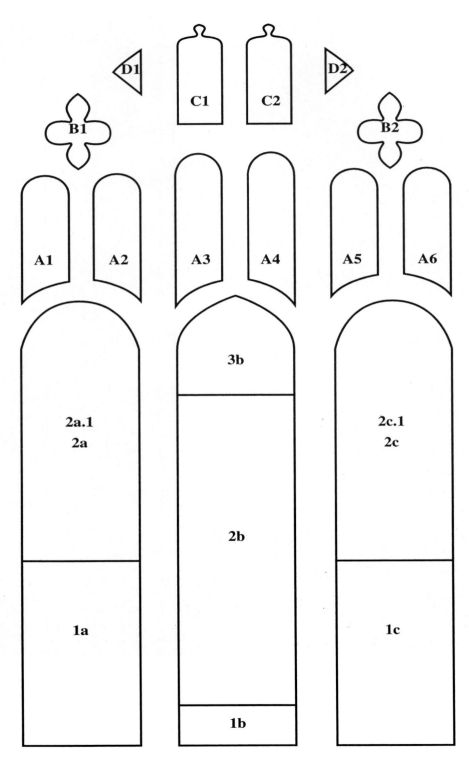

Window **n11**

Window **n11** (RCHME, © Crown Copyright)

Window **n111**

Window **n111** (RCHME, © Crown Copyright)

Window **n1V**

Window **n1V** (RCHME, © Crown Copyright)

Window nV

Window **nV** (RCHME, © Crown Copyright)

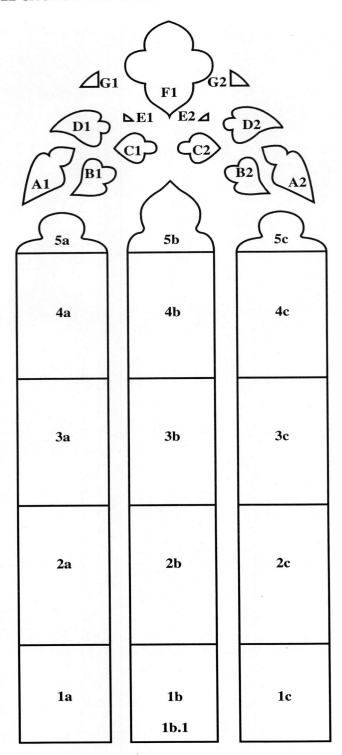

Window **s11**

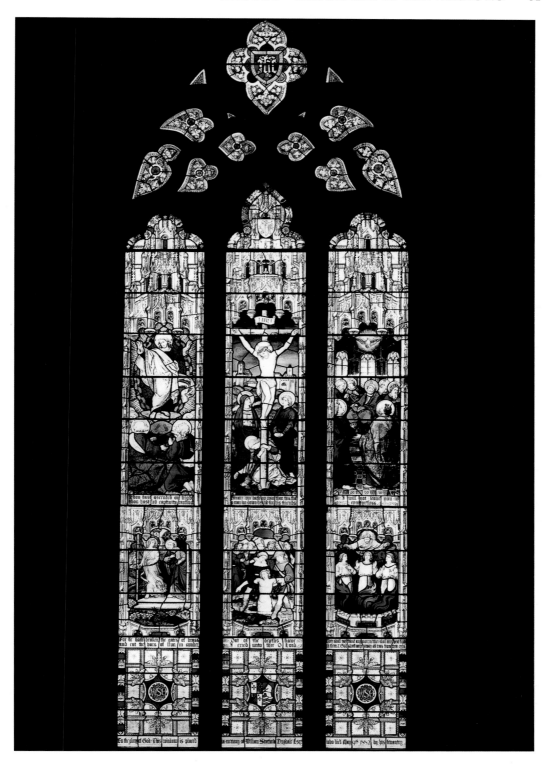

Window **s11**  (RCHME, © Crown Copyright)

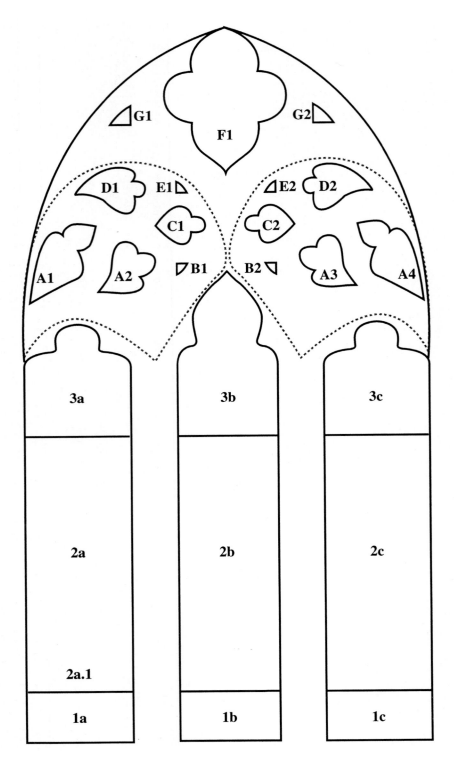

Window **s111**

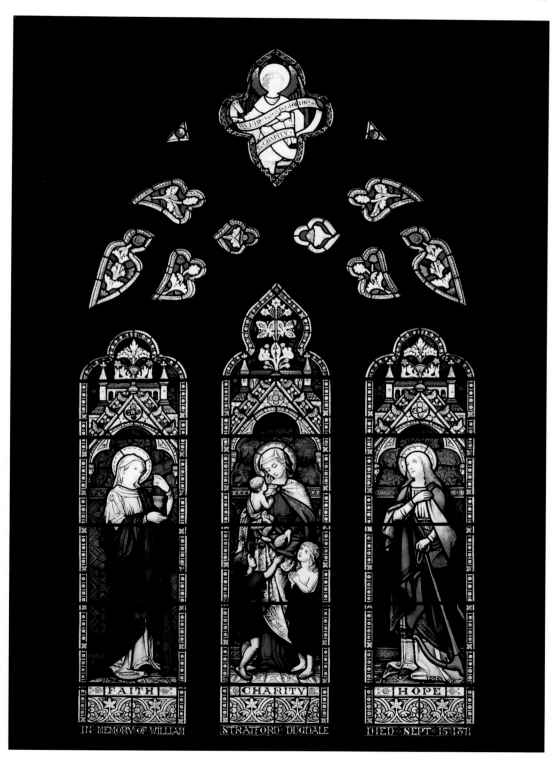

Window **s111**  (RCHME, © Crown Copyright)

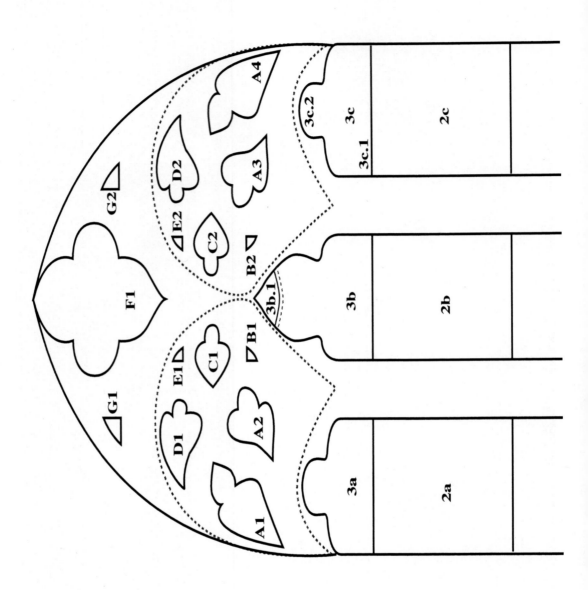

Window s1V

Window **s1V**
(RCHME,
© Crown Copyright)

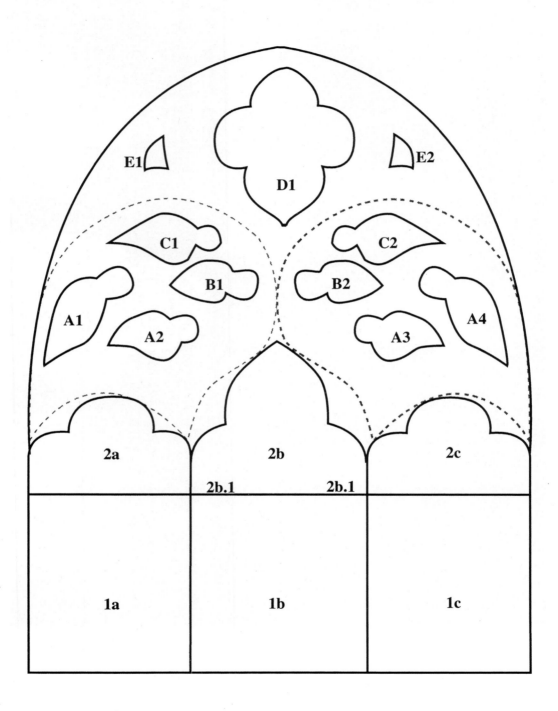

Window **sV**

<u>NOTE</u>

The darkened glass in **sV**
make it impossible to take a
satisfactory photograph

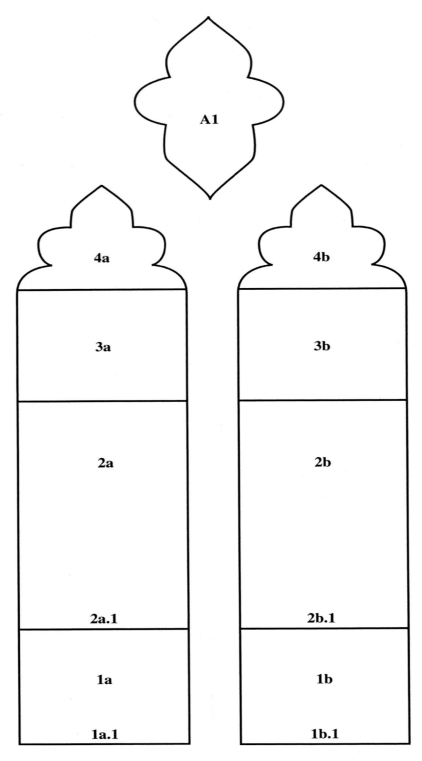

Window **sV1**

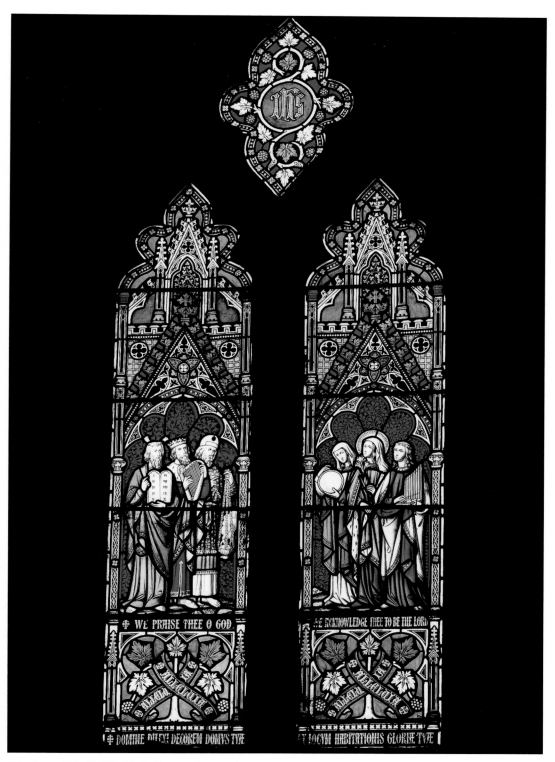

Window **sV1**  (RCHME, © Crown Copyright)

# CHAPTER 4

## *STAINED AND PAINTED GLASS WINDOWS*

In an age of mass communication, with television and radio almost dominating people's lives, when books are printed in their hundreds of thousands, it is difficult to understand the importance of stained glass windows as a means of spreading the Christian Gospel in the Middle Ages. From the very small quantity of medieval glass left in our churches and cathedrals, it is perhaps even more difficult to imagine the enormous numbers of windows that were produced in the four hundred years between the twelfth and the fifteenth centuries. Dr Richard Marks says that the quantity of glass remaining is a 'minute fraction'.[1] Andrew Graham-Dixon says 'Virtually all medieval art in Britain was destroyed between 1536, when Henry VIII dissolved the monasteries, and 1658, when Oliver Cromwell died, effectively bringing the long process of Reformation to a close'.[2] This mass destruction obviously included most of the very best examples of the medieval glazier's art. The enormous loss of quantity is perhaps easier to appreciate than the enormous loss of quality. Compared with Europe who neither had a Dissolution nor a period of wholesale iconoclasm we are, artistically, a thousand times the poorer.   To the ordinary people, certainly illiterate, this glass provided the most effective means of communicating spiritual truths. The windows were their pictorial Bible, their visual aid.

Obviously the majority of windows had religious themes for their subject matter, i.e. scenes from the Old and the New Testaments and from the lives and the miracles of the saints. The genealogy of Christ – the Jesse Window – was a popular subject. From the fourteenth century onwards heraldry and figures of benefactors played a larger part as subject matter.  At Merevale there are numerous references to  the Ferrers family, the Founders of the Abbey, and to the donors.  Dugdale illustrates no less than twenty-two armorial shields in 1656 which include the Earls of Lancaster and Warwick.[3] Of these, only three fragments remain. In fact Merevale glass provides important and positive evidence that at least from the middle of the fourteenth century lay people were giving stained glass to Cistercian houses.[4]

In descriptions of what is commonly called 'stained glass' the expression 'painted glass' is sometimes used. It would be as well to define the difference and at the same time to explain the manufacturing processes in use at this time.

Until the sixteenth century all the coloured glass used in such windows were made from 'pot-metal' sheet glass imported from the continent. The colours were obtained by the addition of  metallic salts in the molten glass. The only English glass manufactured during this period was white. Using a small sketch design, which may have been prepared by the master-glazier himself or obtained from an illuminator of manuscripts, the glass painter made a full-size working drawing of the window, with a black or red line, on a whitened table top.  This cartoon included all the details of the design and the disposition of the lead armature. Different colours were indicated by means of a letter. Having chosen the appropriate sheet of glass, coloured or white, the painter laid it over the drawing. The individual piece was then made by drawing a red-hot iron round the shape required, after starting a crack by dropping water, or more probably spitting on it. The resulting rough piece was then grosed away around the edges with a notched iron until the correct shape and size had been obtained. The notches on the back of a modern glass-cutter are a vestige of this medieval grosing iron, and are put there for the same purpose.

When all the shapes had been cut, they were laid out ready for the painter to trace on  the surface of the glass, the details of the design being seen on the drawing underneath. He did this with a pigment made from copper or iron oxide, mixed with a flux of finely pulverised soft glass and ground with a medium of gum and water, wine or urine. When all the painting was complete, the pieces of glass were laid out on an iron plate previously covered with a fine layer of ash or quicklime, and fired in a kiln. This firing followed every fresh application of paint although it is unlikely that the glass was fired numerous times.

When the firing was complete it only remained to join all the pieces together by means of thin strips of lead of an 'H' section, known as calmes, to smear the joints with suet or resin and to solder them together. When one side was finished the panel was reversed and the other side soldered. The final operation was to force some form of waterproof mastic between the lead and the glass to make the whole panel watertight.

Two more technical discoveries complete this account of the craft during the medieval period. Early in the fourteenth century it was found that by applying a solution of silver salt to the surface of the glass and firing it, the glass was stained a yellow colour varying from a pale lemon-yellow to a deep orange, almost ruby, depending on the strength of the solution and the firing temperature (silver stain fires at a lower temperature than glass paint). The solution was applied to the outside surface of the glass. It revolutionised the art of designing and making stained glass windows.[5] To make a face with yellow hair it was no longer necessary to fix with leading pot-metal yellow glass to white or pinkish glass. One piece of glass could now be used, the hair being stained yellow and the face left clear. Canopies and foliage could be enriched without introducing extra lead lines. Varieties in borders and inscriptions could be produced without much additional trouble or expense. Richness was obtained not at the cost of light but with an increase of it.[6]

The second innovation is the process of abrasion. Ruby (red) glass was made by applying a layer of red glass to a sheet of white. By grinding away parts of the flash, with whetstone and water, the white glass showed through. Two colours could now be made on the same piece of glass. With the addition of the silver stain this could be made three. This was to prove invaluable in making, for instance, heraldic windows where some of the shields had complicated designs on a very small scale.[7] Although examples of abraded ruby have been found in 13th C. windows, it became widely used in the 15th C.

A development from drawing the cartoons on a whitened table was to draw them on large made-up sheets of parchment, and, later, on paper. This had various advantages, for instance they could be rolled up and stored. However they only appear late in the medieval period. Cartoons became the stock-in-trade of a Master Glazier, and were handed down to apprentices. There are records of some cartoons being used for almost a hundred years.

There are many instances of these methods of medieval glass-making at Merevale. Knowledge of these developments is that it helps to establish the date of particular pieces of glass.

A further insight into the method of the construction of windows can be seen at Merevale. In the Prophet Malachi panel (**2a** in **1**) there is a glazier's position mark. It is towards the bottom of the panel, on a piece of orange/brown glass, and is the letter 'P' (**2a.1** in **1**). The final stage was the insertion of the glass panels into the window openings. As a preliminary, numbers, geometric devices or letters were sometimes scratched or painted on the glass for the purpose of ensuring that the panels were inserted in the correct location and order. This practice is common in other medieval crafts. They are found quite frequently, for example, on the backs of English alabaster panels from altarpieces. There is a very similar 'P' mark in fourteenth century glass in the Lady Chapel in Wells Cathedral. There are also glazier's position marks in glass at New College Chapel, Oxford, Winchester College Chapel, Fairford, and King's College Chapel, Cambridge.[8] The marks were also possibly used in the glazing to identify a particular stack of glass in the kiln.

It is hoped that this explanation will assist in interpreting the description of the windows at Merevale.

1    Marks 1993, p xxiv.
2    Graham-Dixon 1996, p 34.
3    Dugdale 1656, p 783.
4    Norton 1986, p 223.
5    Baker 1978, pp 2-3.
6    Woodforde 1954, p 6.
7    Knowles 1925, p 3.
8    Marks 1993, p 37.

# CHAPTER 5

## *THE TREE OF JESSE AND JESSE WINDOWS.*

The prophecy of Isaiah (xi. 1-2) – 'And there shall a rod come out of the stem of Jesse, and a branch shall grow out of his roots: And the spirit of the Lord shall rest upon him' – was given visual interpretation in Christian art in the Middle Ages as the Tree of Jesse. The medieval mind eagerly grasped any opportunity of depicting prefigurations – earlier representations – of Christ and the Virgin in the Old Testament. It can be said therefore that the similarity of the word *virga* meaning a stem or branch, and *virgo* meaning a virgin showed plainly that such an interpretation as the Tree of Jesse was obvious.

This is the usual explanation. It is however an over-simplification. The Old Testament was assiduously searched during the ninth and tenth centuries for such prefigurations. For instance the Immaculate Conception of the Virgin found its figurative expression in the garden enclosed (*hortus conclusus* – Song of Solomon iv. 12), in the gate that was shut (*porta clausa* – Ezekiel xli. 1), in the unspotted mirror (*speculum sine macula* – Wisdom of Solomon. vii. 26), and in other images. The Virgin's prefigurations included the burning bush of Moses (*Rubus igneus* – Exodus iii. 1-6), and seven others including the three *virgea* – stems. These were the stem of Moses (*virga Moysi* – Exodus iv. 1-4), the stem of Aaron (*virga Aaron* – Numbers xvii. 1-7), and the stem of Jesse (*virga Jesse* – Isaiah xi. 1-2). The last was of course a figurative prophecy and was therefore doubly significant. The earliest Trees of Jesse are to be found in manuscripts. These include a Gospel at Prague University Library and a Bible at the Bibliothèque in Dijon, both of the eleventh century. The earliest in the UK. is in a Bible in Lambeth Palace Library c.1140. The first two of these did not include a representation of the Virgin, but the third one did. This is perhaps significant because as the centuries went by the merging of the verbal similarity of *virga* and *Virgo* lent considerable force to the association. It is important to see that this was not just a verbal coincidence but overlapping imagery deeply rooted in theological thought.[1] In this way it will be seen that not only does the Tree of Jesse have a strong symbolism showing the ancestry of Christ with attendant prophets, but that it is also a group of figures that stand for the Virgin herself. The Revised Version reads 'And there shall come forth a shoot out of the stock of Jesse, and a branch out of his roots shall bear fruit'. It can easily be seen that this interpretation would have a profound effect on, for instance, Cistercian monks.

In the fully developed form the figure of Jesse is shown lying down, at the bottom of the design, with a tree springing from his loins. On the vertical axis of the tree are represented the Kings of Judah, the ancestors of Christ, ascending to the Virgin Mary and Christ at the top.   In the side branches of the tree are the prophets of the Old

Testament, the spiritual ancestors of Christ, who foretold the Incarnation and His coming. The textual sources are the Isaiah prophecy and the genealogy of Christ as given by St Matthew (i. 1-17) and St Luke (iii. 23-38). St Matthew lists twenty-six names between David, son of Jesse, and Christ; St Luke lists forty-two. St Matthew's list seems to have been preferred.

It could be mentioned that there are parallels between the Tree of Jesse and Oriental art. This is particularly so in the depictions of the Birth of Brahma where the tree resembles a lotus, and rises from the navel of a recumbent figure culminating in another figure or figures.2 Before discussing the Tree of Jesse as portrayed in stained glass a sideways glance should be taken. In St Mary's Priory Church, Abergavenny, there is a crudely carved and powerfully emotive figure of Jesse. It was hewn out of the trunk of an oak tree late in the fifteenth century. When it was complete it grew from Jesse's groin and twisted up the wall with other figures, culminating with Christ and the Virgin. It must have been an awesome sight. Here we are back firmly in earthy England, the land of pagan cults and Green Men. As Andrew Graham-Dixon says 'The Abergavenny Jesse is an image with roots that clutch. The tree was an ancient focus of fertility cults stretching from Athens to Snowdonia, and the Christian Tree of Jesse was an attempt to appropriate one of the oldest and most powerful pagan symbols and turn it into an agent for the Catholic church'.3 Although it is now a unique form of the Tree of Jesse, there were doubtless many other examples. It just happened that the Abergavenny Jesse escaped the bonfires of the Reformation.

The earliest known representation in stained glass is the magnificent window, now incomplete, in the Abbey of St Denis, near Paris, of 1144. This was soon followed by a related example at Chartres, in 1150. The extent of the St Denis window is uncertain, but it included at least two kings, the Virgin and Christ, and probably eight, or more, prophets. The Chartres Window shows four kings, the Virgin and Christ, and fourteen prophets in addition to Jesse. A figure of a king from a Jesse tree at York Minster is stylistically related to the St Denis and Chartres windows.4

Of the thirteenth century, parts of Jesse windows can be found at Salisbury Cathedral, Lincoln Cathedral, Westwell in Kent, and Kidlington in Oxfordshire.

Of the fourteenth century, there are examples, or fragments, at Selby Abbey, the chapel of Winchester College, Wells Cathedral, New College, Oxford, Tewkesbury Abbey and Gedney in Lincolnshire. Also of this century and dated 1320-1340 there are the remains of six Trees of Jesse in the Midlands. These are at Lowick in Northamptonshire, Shrewsbury, Mancetter, Merevale, Ludlow, Madley in Herefordshire, only the last two of which are perhaps from the same workshop.

Unfortunately all the windows of this Midlands group are incomplete; the overall design of the original windows are therefore unknown. It seems possible though that the tracery lights of each widow may have contained a Christ in Majesty of the Last Judgement, with the dead rising from their graves. 5

The Merevale Jesse most probably came from a West Midland workshop (based in

Oxford ?) that was active c.1330-1350. To this group belongs glass from Hadzor, Kempsey, Worcester Cathedral, and the Latin Chapel of Christ Church, Oxford.

The church at Madley, in Herefordshire, has three lights from a Jesse window. There is an unidentified king, the prophet Ezekiel and King Josiah. They are stylistically closely related to Merevale, but as stated above, not from the same workshop. The church is dedicated to the Nativity of the Blessed Virgin Mary. Before the Reformation there was a statue of the Virgin there, to which pilgrimage was made from the surrounding countryside. This is probably the reason for the size of the building, which is far beyond the needs of an ordinary rural parish.[6] Madley and the gate chapels at Furness and Merevale all have this same story of pilgrimage in common.

The Jesses at Ludlow and Merevale are also stylistically closely related, and the designs of King Manasses and King Asa at Ludlow and King Solomon and King Hezekiah at Merevale appear to be from the same hand. There are also similar squirrels, monkeys and birds. Perhaps the answer lies in a peripatetic craftsman.

The figures of three Kings from a Jesse window at Mancetter have often been thought to be part of the Merevale Jesse. Both the Victoria County History [7] and Pevsner,[8] no less, perpetuate this error. Even a casual look at the glass will show that the treatment of the vine stem is different from Merevale, also the Kings at Mancetter have wiry, jutting-out beards, the bodies are more attenuated and angular, and they stand in slightly dancing poses. They are altogether different from the more static, sitting postures of the Merevale figures.[9] King Jeconiah, at Mancetter, has a scroll inscribed in Lombardic script, whilst all the scrolls at Merevale are in a Black-letter script. Although this is not proof that they are from a different window, it suggests so. If more proof is needed, both windows contain a figure of King David holding his harp. The Mancetter Jesse figures, which have been dated 1320-1340 are thought to be probably from a Midlands glazier's workshop which also made glass that is at Woodborough in Nottingham. The error linking the two Jesse windows is most likely to have occurred because of the connection between the two churches. In 1427 the church of Mancetter was appropriated by the Abbey. In 1458-9 the Abbot, John Riggeley, founded a religious Guild at Mancetter, and had a guild-house built near the church. Mancetter also possibly has one of the Abbey bells – see Appendix G – The Inventory.[10]

Other glass possibly coming from the same workshop can be seen at Fillongley, Warwickshire. In a panel of fragments in a window in the north aisle there are two heads not dissimilar to some at Merevale.

The best preserved and certainly the most striking of this Midlands Jesse group is at Lowick, where there are fifteen kings and prophets. It is thought to be the work of a Master Glazier somewhat isolated in design from the others. It is dated 1320-1330.

Shrewsbury has sixteen kings and prophets but the extensive restoration has been done so well that it is almost impossible to say what is original and what is modern. It can be dated 1340-1353, on the evidence of donor figures at the base of the window.

It should be noted that all the Kings and Prophets in the Merevale Jesse, and in other Jesse windows, are placed among the coils of the vine which have been arranged into compartments of a 'vesica piscis' shape. This name is given to a pointed oval, formed by two equal circles cutting each other in their centres. It was commonly used as an aureole around the Virgin and the Persons of the Trinity in sculpture and paintings in the Middle Ages. It was also common in medieval seals, particularly of bishops and monastic establishments. The name means literally a fishes bladder, and the shape was probably called this because of the early Christian 'fish' symbol. To be more specific, the Kings are represented seated with the branches shaped around them, whilst the Prophets are shown standing with the branches, which they sometimes grasp, coiling around and about them.[11]

Finally, some details should be given of the origin and more recent history of the Merevale Jesse. The absence of the figures of Jesse and the Virgin and the late date of the perpendicular tracery show that the glass is not *in situ*. The original design must have filled a very large widow. The most likely original location is the east window of the abbey church, and the Jesse would certainly have been an appropriate subject. If it were made for a Cistercian church it is a good example of the rejection by the English Cistercians of the prohibition on the Order's use of colours and figured glass, a feeling that was general from the last quarter of the thirteenth century. In a lecture in 1922, Sir William's father said 'By tradition the glass came from the east window of the Choir of the Abbey church. During the Parliamentary wars the window was taken out and buried in the grounds of Merevale Hall. (Possibly near where the kitchen-gardens are now). At the beginning of the last century it was discovered, and pieced together by my great-grandmother (Charlotte Curzon, died 1832) and her sister.'[12] This would imply that the window remained in the conventual church for one hundred years. For all this time it would have been in a building with no roof, as the lead was stripped off immediately after the Dissolution. The Abbey buildings were a vast quarry of ready-cut stone for sale. The Dissolution was the officially sanctioned starting-point for more than a century of iconoclasm in England, although the ideas of reformation had already been fermenting in Europe for many years. The radical leaders of the new Protestant church were vigorous and determined opponents of all Roman Catholic rituals and imagery.[13] However there were times towards the end of Henry VIII's reign when a slight conservatism crept in, and of course there was Mary's reign when Roman Catholicism staged a come-back. As early as 1525 even Zwingli said 'We do not think those images should be pulled down which were placed in windows purely for the sake of ornament, for then nobody worships in such a place'. In her Statutes of the 1560s and later, Elizabeth sometimes imposed a restraining hand on iconoclasm, particularly of stained glass.[14] However it is still remarkable that the Merevale Jesse survived. The iconoclasts often destroyed a single figure in a group, or even just the head of a figure. It is therefore perhaps not surprising that what has been lost includes the figures of Christ and the Virgin Mary, as well as Jesse.

It could be suggested that Sir William perhaps implied that the glass was taken out of the Gate Chapel, not the Abbey, at the time of the Civil War and buried. This would be on the assumption that it had been removed from the Abbey earlier, after the Dissolution, and placed in the Gate Chapel, along with the brass effigy (**M9**), the inscised slabs (**M5** and **M26**), the Rood Screen and possibly the tomb-chest (**M39**). The end result however does not make a lot of difference.

The glass was buried, it is said, in lead-lined boxes. It is difficult to imagine how it was 'pieced together' by Mrs Charlotte Dugdale and her sister. However, in 1850, under the supervision of Henry Clutton, the remains of the window were incorporated in the East window.[15] In total there are now fifteen figures, of which the five in the bottom row are modern (**1a, 1b, 1c, 1d** and **1e**). They are by Ward and Hughes who carried out what might be called the second restoration. This was in about 1872. William Stratford Dugdale had died in 1871, and Ward and Hughes were commissioned to make a memorial window (**s111**). The design of the Jesse window was adapted in 1873 for a new great west window which Ward and Hughes made for St George's, Doncaster. It is one of several instances of Victorian glass painters 'lifting' medieval designs in this way.[16] Of the remaining 10 figures, that of Christ in Majesty (**3b**) is 15thC glass and has been inserted from elsewhere. Also it should be noted that perhaps King David (**2b**) is on a smaller scale.

In 1890 the church underwent a major restoration (see monument **M16**). It would appear the whole building was on the verge of collapse. The piers of the north and south arcades were tilted and apparently 'tumbling about in an alarming manner.' The condition became so dangerous that the church was elaborately shored up, both internally and externally, by timbers.[17] The entire roof was taken off, and the Jesse window temporarily removed,[18] presumably for safety. In 1939 the glass was partially releaded by Mr John Hudston. Quotations have been received (1997) from York Glazier's Trust for complete cleaning and restoration, and iso-thermal protection.

1    Watson 1934, p 45.
2    Watson 1934, p 68.
3    Graham-Dixon 1996, p 25.
4    Newton 1961, p 301.
5    Newton 1961, p 304.
6    Madley n.d., p1.
7    Salzman IV 1947, p 124.
8    Pevsner Warwickshire 1974, p 346.
9    Prof. Marks, in conversation with the author.
10   Mairs 1982, pps 3-4.
11   Newton 1961, p 302.
12   Dugdale 1922, p 3.
13   Graham-Dixon 1996, p 16.
14   Aston 1988, Chapter 6.
15   Welsh 1973, p 8.
16   Harrison 1980, p 38.
17   Birmingham Mercury 21 November 1891.
18   Photograph taken by W.S.F.D in Sept. 1890.

# CHAPTER 6

## *NOTE ON MONUMENTS*

It is difficult, if not impossible, to write anything about monuments or a country churchyard without thinking about Gray's Elegy -

> 'Beneath those rugged elms, that yew-tree's shade
> Where heaves the turf in many a mould'ring heap
> Each in his narrow cell for ever laid
> The rude forefathers of the hamlet sleep.'

As with T. S. Eliot, in the Preface, if it had not been Stoke Poges that had inspired Gray, it could have been Merevale, or a thousand other country churchyards. Since their establishment they have been sanctuaries for the living as well as the dead. Gray's poem is a bitter-sweet piece, a hymn to human frailty and the sacrifices of the rural poor. Its lasting impression, however, is of the continuity and resilience of life: an owl calls from the ivy, a beetle drones, cattle drift slowly past – all glimpsed exactly as they might have been generations before. Life goes on.

Notes follow on some of the various types of memorial listed in the <u>Catalogue of Memorials</u> –

*Brasses*
The origin of the use of brasses may perhaps be accounted for in the following way. Marble monuments, with their carved canopies and life-sized figures, took up a lot of space. Effigies in low relief, placed on the floor, were in the way, and, like incised slabs, liable to wear. During the thirteenth century monumental brasses came into use , following the incised slab in treatment, and were at once cheap, convenient and durable. The material used was an alloy of copper and zinc, called latten. It is a remarkably hard metal, which resists all attempts at disfigurement. Until the middle of the sixteenth century it was manufactured chiefly at Cologne. It was beaten into rectangular sheets and imported into England, hence the name Cullen plates.[1] It is of interest that in the inventory of the Abbey, taken at the Dissolution, there were 'ii candelstykes of latten valued at 5s, and one lampe of latten 8d.' The matrices referred to in the description of **M9** were shallow recesses cut into the stone to take the brass. This is why **M9**, which has no matrices, must have been re-laid at some time on new stone. There is one last matter. Sometimes the word 'palimpsest' is used in connection with brasses. This comes from the Greek meaning 'written again', and was used when a parchment was scraped clean and used again, like a slate. When a brass has been turned over and engraved on the other side it is known as a palimpsest. This happened, for instance, after the Dissolution when the monastic brasses were sold and, sometimes, turned over and used again. In the inventory at Merevale there were 'vi gravestones wyth brass in them.' Perhaps most of these were melted down, but some might still lie in Midland churches with Tudor engravings on the backs. One of them, **M9**, survived intact.

*Alabaster*

The quality of the material obviously dictated the character and quality of the monument. The fine texture of the oolitic limestone contributes to the excellence of **M18**. Alabaster is one of the softest stones to carve and its use for monuments began as early as 1300, becoming popular from about 1350. Its value lay in its suitability for carving the finest details. In later centuries its softness has also made it an easy target for graffiti vandals.  Most alabaster of quality came from quarries at Chellaston near Nottingham. The first documentary evidence of the use of alabaster is of particular interest. In 1374 John of Gaunt sent his agent to the alabaster quarries on his Tutbury estate (by coincidence, previously owned by the Ferrers family)  for six cart loads of alabaster. These were for a tomb in Old St Pauls for his wife, Dame Blanche. The agent was told that if he could not get suitable stone he should obtain it from the quarries at Chellaston, twenty miles away, which was famous for its large blocks as well as its quality. The material was to be selected by the bearer of the letter, evidently a representative of the sculptor.[2]  No doubt the stone for **M39** was obtained in a very similar way.  There is a tomb-chest of Sir Hugh Willoughby and his wife (of 1445) at Willoughby-in-the-Wolds that is comparable with Merevale (c.1440), and it is probable that they both were made in Nottingham. The angels on the sides are of the characteristic Chellaston type. This may be explained by there being a frequent interchange of ideas between the two places. Most probably the best of the Chellaston craftsmen moved to the town, where opportunities for business were better and where the river Trent provided water transport, or perhaps the Chellaston shop was an offshoot of those at Nottingham.[3]

*Hatchments*

Hatchments are a familiar sight in parish churches. They are not only decorative, but of great interest to the herald, the genealogist and local historian. The diamond-shaped hatchment, which originated in the Low Countries, is a debased form of the medieval achievement – the shield, the helm, and other accoutrements carried at the funeral of a noble or knight. It was customary for the hatchment to be hung outside the house during the period of mourning, and then be placed in the church. This custom, begun in the early seventeenth century, is not entirely obsolete, about eighty examples have been recorded in the twentieth century.[4]

It is easy, even at a glance, to gather some information about the person to whom they refer. For instance, if there are two coats-of-arms together (impaled) on a shield it is for a married man, and if on a diamond (lozenge) it is for a married woman. The background is black on the left side (dexter) if the husband has died, and on the right side (sinister) if it is the wife. It is white on the side of whoever is alive. It follows that  of the two hatchments in the north aisle, **M7** is for a married man whose wife was still alive, and **M15** is for a married woman whose husband had predeceased her. In the nave there is a hatchment, **M38**, for a married man whose wife was still alive, but they had both been married before. This is a little more complicated.

1   Macklin 1963,  p 15.
2   Chatwin 1921,  p.33.
3   Chatwin 1921, p 60.
4   Summers 1974,  p x.

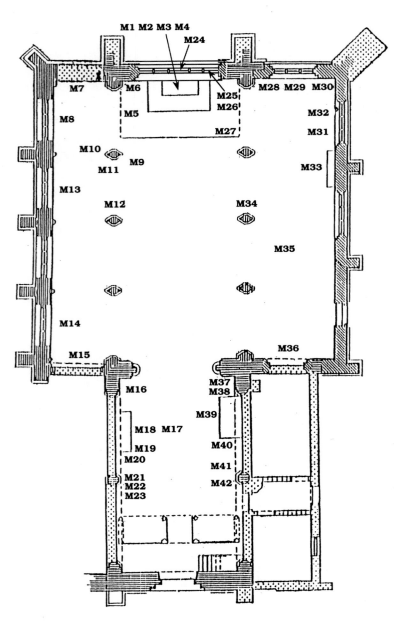

*Plan of Monuments*

# CHAPTER 7

## *CATALOGUE OF MONUMENTS*

Monuments are 'written records of anything that serves to commemorate'. There follows a complete catalogue of every written record in the church and every name in the churchyard. It could be said that these are the most permanent record that there is of anyone who, in any way, has had some connection with this church. It is obviously not a complete account because so many names go unrecorded. The names range over the centuries from the 4th Earl Ferrers who died in 1254, and whose effigy is in the nave, to the most recent addition to the churchyard.

The names are also included of people connected with the church whose names are not actually recorded in the building. They include the names of Abbots, of some of the monks, and of Incumbents.

The monuments in the Church are numbered in an order that is similar to the C.V.M.A. system used for the glass. Those in the east of the chancel are listed first, followed by those on the north side of the chancel and then the nave, starting in the east. There follow the monuments on the south side of the chancel and nave, going also from east to west. The words on the monuments are printed in **bold.** See diagram for the position of the Monuments in the church. All the names in the text and also in the descriptions of the windows, which are in capitals, will be found in the general index.

The Names in the Churchyard include a reference date. The position of the grave will be found on contacting the Rector or a church officer.

## THE EAST, AND THE NORTH SIDE OF THE CHURCH

**M1**    Two brass altar vases. **'Merevale Church. In memory of ANNIE PARDON FEATHERSTONE 1959'**.

**M2**    Book of Common Prayer. including Administration of the Sacraments. Large paper, large print copy, OUP. Label inside front cover reads **'Given in grateful memory of  SHEILA ARMBRISTER by her family and friends. May 1988'**.

**M3**    Two brass candlesticks. **'To the Glory of God and in memory of SAMUEL NEALE, organist of Merevale Church for 48 years. Died 5th January 1926'**. He was schoolmaster at Bentley.

**M4**    Two brass offertory plates. On the reverse of each **'The gift of E.P.M'** and **'The gift of H.D.M'**.

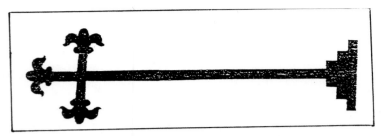

*Incised slab c. 1350 – monuments* **M5** *and* **M26**

**M5**   Incised slab. A Latin cross fleury, ie. the arms are terminated by fleur-de-lis. The cross stands on a Calvary base of three steps. Extremely worn, the design has been almost obliterated. An almost identical slab lies in the centre of the nave at Jervaulx Abbey, except that there are only two steps at the base. There is also a very similar inscised slab in the Leicester Museum and Art Gallery. This was originally in Wyggeston Chantry House and has been dated 1349. **M26**   is identical and also very worn. A date of c.1350 for these slabs ties in with that of the 'Nottingham' group of floor tiles nearby in the chancel, and also the building of the south aisle of the chancel. See illustration.

**M6**   Processional Cross. Presented by Miss Elizabeth Morgan in memory of her mother and father, the Rev. and Mrs H. R. B. MORGAN.

**M7**   Hatchment. Dexter background black. STRATFORD impaling PACKE, as **M15**, but cinquefoil argent. Crest: An arm embowed in armour proper, in a hand a scimitar argent hilted or. Mantling: Gules and argent. Motto: **'Mors janua vitae'** (Death is the start of life). Skull and crossed-bones below shield.
For FRANCIS STRATFORD, who married ANNA, daughter of CLIFTON PACKE of Prestwold, and died 1762.

**M8**   Window. **'In memory of ROBERT JENNINGS. Given by STEPHEN and MARY ELLEN SCOTT'**. See window **nll**.

**M9**   Brasses. They are of ROBERT, Earl FERRERS, of Chartley, died 1412, and his wife MARGARET. The inscription, now lost, is given by Dugdale (1656 p.783). It reads **'Die jacet Robertus Ferrarus de Chartley, qui obiit in die Gregory Pape, anno domini MCCCCX11 et Margareta uxor eius'**. There is also no canopy, and as the brasses, both of which have been broken, and re-laid in a new stone, there are no matrices. It may have been one of the 'vi. grave stones with brass in them' in the Abbey church at the time of the Dissolution.
   The knight is 5ft. 2in. high, and is clad in plate-armour of the early part of the fifteenth century, viz.: bascinet, gorget (instead of the mail camail), epaulieres, brassarts fastened with straps, coutes, vambraces, gauntlets showing the

finger-tips and armed with gadlings, cuisses, genouillieres, jambs, sollerets, and rowelled spurs.  At the armpits are circular plates called roundels which served to cover the joints of the harness.  The breast-plate has a skirt of seven overlapping taces, to the lowermost of which at its centre are fastened three smaller plates forming the baguette.  Below this skirt is a row of rings, every third ring having another depending from it.  This edging of mail may be part of a mail shirt, but is probably merely a survival in the shape of a fringe.  The knight's sword has a straight cross-guard (part of which is lost) and is fastened to an ornamental belt, arranged diagonally across the hips.  Part of a dagger remains at the left side, and the scabbards of this and the sword are ornamented with the usual rows of guttes or drops.  The knight's head rested upon a tilting-helmet, which is lost; the panache of peacock's feathers which adorn it is, however, in good preservation.  At the feet of the effigy is an animal perhaps resembling a bear, but it has been described as a puzzle to both antiquarians and naturalists.  It is a symbol of bravery.  The lady's effigy measures 5ft., and is at the knight's left hand, the head resting on two cushions.  She wears the crespine head-dress, which confined the hair in a net, and formed two small bunches over the ears, the whole being kept in place by a band encircling the head.  Over this is thrown a kerchief.  The rest of the costume is a long mantle fastened across the chest by a cord, and a tightly-fitting kirtle, with tight sleeves reaching to the knuckles and buttoned beneath the forearm with eighteen buttons.  A small dog, with a collar of bells, is at the lady's feet.[1] The dog is a symbol of fidelity.

[1]    Badger 1895, p 80.

**M10**  Brass plate. On pew door. **'HENRY RICHARDSON of Derby 1810'**

**M11**  Brass plaque. Attached to choir-stall. **'In memory of THOMAS B.CLARKE who was a chorister in this church from 1852 to 1919. This tablet was erected by his friends'.**

**M12**  Oak carved inscription. On the choir-stall. **'In memory of SIDNEY DUGDALE (for 25 years the respected and beloved agent of the Dugdale Family Estates) who died September 29th, 1899 aged 53 years. These choir seats were erected by the subscription of 230 friends of all classes'.**

**M13**  Window. Possibly in memory of THOMAS SKEVINGTON, monk of Merevale, and later Abbot of Beaulieu and Bishop of Bangor. See details on window **n111**. Window **n1V** has been associated with JOHN HANDEWELL, chief magistrate of Coventry, and possibly contained his memorial inscription. See details on window **n111**.

**M14**  <u>Window</u>. 'To the Glory of God, and in loving memory of WILLIAM EDWARD MINION, born April 26th 1824, died January 18th 1879'. See window **nV.**

**M15**  <u>Hatchment</u>. All black background. On a lozenge. Barry azure and argent a lion rampant gules (STRATFORD), impaling , Qly sable and or in the dexter chief a cinquefoil or (PACKE). Motto: '**In coelo quies'.** (There is rest in heaven). Cherub's head above lozenge and skull and crossed bones below.
For ANNA, daughter of  CLIFTON PACKE of Prestwold, and widow of FRANCIS STRATFORD. (Died  1779).

**M16**  <u>Brass plaque on wall</u>. '**To the Glory of God AD. 1892. This ancient church had fallen into such an unsafe condition as to require immediate reparation. This was done under the direction of Alfred BICKERDIKE, Architect, during the incumbency of The Rev HUGH BACON, M.A. by whom the church was re-opened for divine service May 25th 1893.'**

**M17**  <u>Inscised slab</u>. '**C.E.B'**

**M18**  <u>Effigy of a Knight</u>, Material: a fine oolite.[1] The figure lies on a flat rectangular slab, but it is much mutilated. Pevsner states that this is one of the earliest monumental records in the county. He describes it as 'exceptionally beautiful, and of the very highest quality.'[2] It is generally presumed to be of William, Fourth Earl Ferrers of Chartley. He was born 1193 and died 9th April, 1254. The manner of his death is curious. He was being carried on a kind of chariot because of his gout but whilst crossing the bridge at St Neots, as a result of the carelessness of the driver, he fell off and was killed. As Patron of the Abbey he was buried in the Chapter House.

The effigy had been buried, perhaps at the time of the Civil War, as was the Jesse window. It was found in Merevale Park early in the nineteenth century and placed in this church. In Mr W.S.Dugdale's MS. Diary, at Merevale Hall, the entry for 9th October, 1848 reads 'Cold frosty N.W. wind. Mr Clutton and Mr Gresley busy excavating the chancel of the Conventual Church. Part of the Founder's leg was found, in chain armour, which fits the figure lying in the Ante-chapel, and identifies it as that of the Founder'. Mr Clutton was Henry Clutton the architect and assistant to Henry Blore who re-built Merevale Hall 1838-1840, excavated the Abbey site, restored the Church, designed the Gate House and the archway. He also built Baddesley Ensor Church. Mr Gresley was the Rev. W. Gresley, Prebendary of Lichfield Cathedral, and author of 'The Forest of Arden, A Tale Illustrative of the English Reformation', published in 1849. It is a novel based on the last years of Merevale Abbey. Mr Dugdale wrote that it was the Founder's leg that they found. In fact the founder of the Abbey

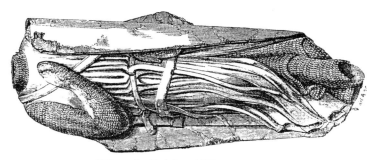

*Effigy of a Knight c.1250 – **M18***

was Robert, Earl Ferrers, and grandfather of William. The piece of leg was attached to the rest of the monument.

The figure consists of little more than the torso, the head and the lower parts of the legs having been lost. The legs are crossed right over left. The armour is all chain mail with rings set edgewise – see the introduction to Monuments. It consists of the hauberk or tunic of mail, with chausses or close fitting pantaloons, also of mail. The hands are protected by mufflers, there are no separate divisions for the fingers, but that for the thumb is plainly shown. The right arm and hand are lying on the breast, the left hand appears beneath the shield, hanging down on the left side. Over the hauberk is a long sleeveless surcoat of linen, belted about the waist with a narrow strap or buckle. Another strap or guige, somewhat broader, to which the shield is attached, crosses diagonally over the right shoulder to the left side. The shield which is on the left side is unusually long – not less than 3ft 9ins – extending from the shoulder to the knee. It is convex in section and in outline it is heater-shaped. The position of the sword is a little odd. It is on the right side and fastened to a belt crossing from the right hip to just below the left hip. It may be because the figure is shown slightly turned on the left side that the sword appears on the right. It is carved as being flat on the slab; it was actually carried at the back. The effigy is very similar to two of the oldest effigies in the Temple Church, London, which also have a long shield and the windswept arrangement of the drapery of the surcoat.[3] Bloxam agrees with the connection with William, Earl Ferrers, but dates it c.1225. He writes 'This effigy considered by itself, I should take to have been executed some thirty years earlier than the time of his death (1254), but there is no one else to whom I can assign it'.[4] Pevsner dates it to the second half of the thirteenth century, which makes more sense if it does commemorate William. This effigy is not mentioned by Dugdale, because it was not in the church in 1656.

1    Chatwin 1921, p 36.
2    Pevsner, Warwickshire p.353
3    Bloxam 1864, p 2.
4    Bloxam 1864, p 6.

**M19**  Brass War Memorial Plaque    'To the Glory of God and in ever grateful memory of the following who laid down their lives in the Great War.
Private G. CRAIG, Seaforth Highlanders.
Private W. FOSTER, Royal Worcestershire Regt.
Private J. HIGGINSON, Royal Worcestershire Regt.
Sapper C. HOUNDSLOW, Royal Engineers,
Private A. MITCHELL, Royal Warwickshire Regt.
Private A. OXFORD, Royal Warwickshire Regt.
Private H. TAYLOR, Royal Warwickshire Regt.
            'Their names shall live for ever'.


**M20**  Mural Tablet.
'In a vault adjoining
Are deposited the mortal remains
of MARY the beloved wife of
RICHARD INGE Esq. of Benn Hill
in this parish ,
Also those of the above named
RICHARD INGE Esq.
Son of the Revd WILLIAM INGE
Canon Residentiary
Of Lichfield Cathedral:
Who was grandson of WILLIAM INGE Esq.
of Thorpe Constantine
in the County of Stafford:
He died January 7th 1841.
In the same vault lies interred
SOPHIA ELIZABETH
Grand-daughter of the above:
and eldest child of
The Revd CHARLES INGE M.A.
And MARY ANNE, his wife,
She died August 23rd 1842,
Aged 17.'


**M21**  Commemorative stone N.Z. **'Presented by Merevale  Church, N.Z. 1956'.** The beginning of the connection between this church and that of the same name in New Zealand began in the early years of the nineteenth century.  Two sons of Rev. Robert Harrington (Incumbent of  this church 1780-1795) emigrated to New Zealand, under the Canterbury Settlement scheme, sponsored by the Church to settle young Englishmen in the colonies, and settled in undeveloped country north of Christchurch.  They named their land Merevale after the Dugdale estate on which they had spent their childhood.

The first church of St Mary  was consecrated in 1866.  It was a wooden structure, 58 feet long and 18 feet wide, and situated on Papanui Road which was unpaved and dusty, running between sparse houses and open countryside. In the early days, although the church was well attended, finance was difficult and there were many problems.  However, in 1928 a fine new church was built, using Otago granite.  Amongst other things it contains the largest organ in any parish church in New Zealand.  In 1936 the Archdeacon of Christchurch, the Rev. A. K. Warren, came to England and visited this church. He met Sir William Dugdale's father, who had visited the original church in 1898 when he was twenty-six, and who told him the history of Merevale Abbey. He was given a block of stone from the Abbey.  The 'Atherstone News' of 13th November, 1936 had an article the headline of which was 'Romance of Stone's 12,000 Miles Journey'. "In the hold of a liner which steamed out of Southampton yesterday," it read, "bound on its 12,000 mile voyage to New Zealand  there was a block of stone taken out of the nave of Merevale Church, Atherstone, and is to be placed in the porch of St Mary's, Merivale, Christchurch, New Zealand."  (The change of spelling came about in around 1900).   The article went on to describe how Archdeacon Warren, "a tall young cleric, spoke of his appointment to St Mary's, Merivale, and how he often wondered how his parish was so named."  It gave the history "of the ancient glories of what is known as the Chapel of Our Lady Beyond the Gate," much of which Archdeacon Warren later related to his parish. In 1956 a visitor from St Mary-in-Merivale returned the compliment by presenting this commemorative stone, of Otago granite.

The present vicar of St Mary-in-Merivale, on the corner of Papanui Road and Merivale Lane which is now a major suburb of Christchurch, is the Rev Blair Robertson.  He has sent a history of his church, published on the occasion of their centenary in 1966.  It contains a photograph of this church and a brief history of the Abbey; they obviously look on us as their 'mother-church'.  He is eager to establish a link between the two congregations. There is a photograph of  St Mary-in-Merivale hanging in the nave of this church near the stone. The visit of Mr and Mrs David Cox to N. Z. in March 1997 helped promote this relationship.

**M22** <u>Framed Document</u>. **'Pilgrimage to Merevale 1361. On July 30th 1361 ROBERT de STRETTON, Bishop of Coventry and Lichfield, wrote to THOMAS of LEICESTER, a monk at Merevale Abbey, arranging for absolution to be granted to pilgrims dying at the Abbey. Although the Black Death is not explicitly mentioned, there is little doubt that it was the spur of the Pilgrimage. Two days after this letter was written the bishop ordered penitential processions to avert the plague which, although it had not entered his diocese, had emptied other parts of the kingdom.**

Below is a photograph of the original letter, reproduced by kind permission of the Lichfield Record Office and the Lichfield Diocesan Registrar (LJRO:B/A/iif.43v.) Beneath the letter, which is in Latin, is a translation.'

There follows the Bishop's letter.

'We see it as our Pastoral duty to extend our patronage in matters which concern the health of souls. We have been told that a great multitude of the faithful, for the expiation of their offences, pour almost daily to the Chapel built beside the gateway of your monastery which is dedicated to the praise and honour of the most glorious Virgin Mary, The Mother of God, and we have further gathered, by the testimony of people of credence, that it often happens that many of our subjects, both men and women, travelling there away from home, are brought to the point of death by the crush of people or by falling sick of the various illnesses prevalent in these days.

We wish to make provision for the spiritual health of these people and accordingly (having complete faith in your circumspection and the sedulous affection which you are known to have towards the health of men's souls) we give you full and unlimited power to absolve those of our subjects who, while on Pilgrimage to the aforesaid Chapel, find themselves at the point of death and wish to make full confession to you, and to impose a salutary penance upon them according to the nature of their fault. This power is also to extend to cases normally reserved to us, and is to last as long as we decide'.

'Presented by the Friends of the Church of Our Lady, Merevale, Good Friday 1997.'

It is interesting to note that the 'second wave' of the Black Death raged in England in the summer of 1361, particularly in Warwickshire.

**M23**   Hatchment. All black background. Qly, 1st and 4th, Or on a chevron vert three leopards facing argent (INGE), 2nd and 3rd, Azure on a chevron engrailed between them three lions passant guarding or three crosses moline sable (FOWLER), impaling, Fowler
Crest: Two battle-axes in satire proper enfiled with a ducal coronet or
Mantling: Gules and argent.
Motto: **'Ne Cede malis'** (Do not concede to evil).

For RICHARD INGE of Shrewsbury, who married MARY, daughter of THOMAS FOWLER of Pendeford, and died 1784.


## THE EAST AND THE SOUTH SIDE OF THE CHURCH

**M24**   Piece of glass. The name **'JOHN SMITH'** is scratched in the centre of King Solomon's right hand in **2c.1**. The signature of the glazier?

**M25**  Brass offertory plate. On the front: **'To do good and to distribute, forget not.'** On the reverse: **'Bentley 1887 Jubilee'.** The Church of St John, Bentley, was built 1837 and demolished 1971.

**M26**  Incised slab. Identical to **M5**. Very worn, the design has almost gone. c.1350.

**M27**  Two Sanctuary Chairs.  From Bentley Church, in 1971. The X-shaped legs are joined by crossbars held together by wooden pins, and the flat arms are joined to the back  in the same way. The design is known as 'Glastonbury' from two early medieval chairs, one of which is in St John's Church, Glastonbury, and the other in the Bishop's Palace, Wells.

**M28**  Mural Tablet. **'In loving memory of ALICE FRANCES wife of WILLIAM STRATFORD DUGDALE daughter of Sir CHARLES TREVELYAN, Bart of Wallington, who died January 2nd 1902. This tablet is placed here by her two sons'.**

**M29**  Window. **'To the Glory of God this window is placed in memory of WILLIAM STRATFORD DUGDALE., who died May 9th 1882, by his tenantry'.** See window **s11**.

**M30**  Tablet. Situated high on wall. **'Underneath are deposited the remains of FRANCIS STRATFORD Esqre, of the Manor of Merevale in the County of Leicester and Warwick who departed this life 22nd day of August 1762 aged 57. He married ANN the youngest daughter of CLIFTON PACKE of Prestwold in the said County of Leicester. Likewise he had a son named JAMES who died as an infant and was here interred, and four surviving daughters PENELOPE BATE, SARAH  ANNA, FRANCISCA and MARIA. He was a man of few faults and blessed with many virtues. Here also lieth the body of ANN STRATFORD wife of the above FRANCIS STRATFORD Esq., who with unremitting affection to the memory of her late husband survived him 17 years and died the 29th day of September 1779 in the 77th year of her age. Segnites Inimica Gloria'.** (Idleness is the enemy of Glory).

**M31**  Window. **'In Memory of WILLIAM STRATFORD DUGDALE'.** See window **s111**.

**M32**  Piece of Glass. Signed by the artist **'H. HUGHES** London 1872' of Ward and Hughes, (see Appendix C). See **2a.1** in window **s111**.

**M33**  <u>Large Mural Tablet</u>.

'Sacred to the Memory of
DUGDALE STRATFORD DUGDALE Esqre.
of Merevale Hall in the County of Warwick,
who departed this life
November 5th AD. 1836
in the 64th year of his age.
He was the only surviving son of
RICHARD GEAST DUGDALE Esqre
of Blythe Hall in the same County,
by PENELOPE BATE,
eldest daughter and heiress of
FRANCIS STRATFORD Esqre of Merevale.
He married first AD. 1799
the Honble CHARLOTTE CURZON,
youngest daughter of ASSHETON,
1st Viscount CURZON,
by whom he had one son,
and secondly, AD. 1834,
MARY ELIZABETH
widow of Sir MARK SYKES Bart,
and daughter of WILLIAM EGERTON Esqre
of Tatton Park, Cheshire,
by whom he had no issue.
For twenty nine years
he served his native county in Parliament
with un-wearied diligence and fidelity,
and in all the relations of public and private life,
he sought to glorify God,
endeavouring to promote the happiness of his fellow creatures.
Also in the same vault are deposited
the remains of his first wife,
The Hon CHARLOTTE DUGDALE,
who died December 30th 1832
in the 61st year of her age.
The monument is erected
to the memory of his beloved parents,
by their devoted son
WILLIAM STRATFORD DUGDALE.
Beneath, in the same vault by the side of his Father and Mother
repose the mortal remains of
WILLIAM STRATFORD DUGDALE.
He was born at Merevale April 1st 1800
and died at Blythe Hall September 15th 1871.

He married March 1st 1827,
HARRIET ELLA youngest daughter of
EDWARD B. PORTMAN Esqre of Bryanston, County Dorset
and by her had issue seven sons and three daughters,
of whom six sons and two daughters survive him.
"He lived loving and loved.
Goodness and he fill up one monument."
In the neighbouring churchyard,
by the side of her youngest son SIDNEY
repose the mortal remains of the above named
HARRIET ELLA DUGDALE.
She died on the 17th April 1903 aged 93 years and 355 days,
having been blessed with the full possession of her faculties unto the end'
"Here are they that keep the Commandment of God
and the faith of Jesus." Rev xiv.: 12.'

**M34** <u>Brass Plaque on back of Choirstalls</u>. '**In memory of SIDNEY DUGDALE for 25 years the respected and beloved agent of the Dugdale Family Estates who died September 29th 1899 aged 53 years. These choir seats were erected by the subscriptions of 230 friends of all ranks'**.

**M35** <u>The Organ</u>. Made in 1777 by John Snetzler, who was born in Germany but spent his working life in England. It has a signed label inside the case which reads '**JOHANNES SNETZLER fecit Londini 1777'**.

It is a substantial organ of the 'wreathed-oval design' type and was almost certainly made for Merevale Hall. The organ maker James Bishop supplied a new organ to the Hall in 1836, at the time when the hall was being rebuilt, and it is thought that this instrument came to the church then. The mahogany case has lost its 'broken' pediment and some carvings, its roof, its doors, and two dummy pipes of the 'oval'; the kneeboard also appears to have been replaced, probably when the original wind system was also replaced by a compensated double-rise horizontal reservoir with feeders. The key action has been remade, and at some time the compass reduced to C in the bass. A twenty-note Bourdon with small pedalboard was added. The stop-knobs are not original and are probably of the 1830s. An almost identical instrument but complete with its glass doors etc. can be seen in the City of London church of St Andrew-by-the-Wardrobe. It was made in 1769 for Lord Hatherton of Teddesley Hall, Staffordshire and it has been at St Andrews since 1961.[1]

The organ was renovated in 1973 by Hill, Norman and Beard Ltd. Dr Alan Barnes, who lives locally, is the authority on Snetzler organs and has written the definitive work on them.

---

[1]    Barnes 1994, p 171.

**M36** <u>Small Brass plate</u>. **'Presented by The Rev. B. ASTLEY, Incumbent, from Michaelmas 1856 to Michaelmas 1872.'** The plate is on the sill immediately below window **sV1** and cannot be seen from ground level. See window **sV1**.

**M37** <u>Plaque on wall</u>. **'The clock was presented to this church by HENRY DIGBY PARRY-MITCHELL in the year 1913'.**

**M38** <u>Hatchment</u>. Dexter background black.   A shield and a lozenge.  Shield: Qly 1st & 4th Argent a cross flory gules charged with a king of arms coronet or, in the first quarter a roundel gules (DUGDALE), 2nd and 3rd Barry of ten argent and azure a lion rampant gules (STRATFORD) impaling two coats per pale: dexter Qly, 1st & 4th Argent on a bend sable three popinjays or collared gules (CURZON) 2nd & 3rd Argent two lions passant guardant azure (HANMER) and Sinister, Argent a lion rampant gules between three pheons sable (EGERTON).
Lozenge: Qly 1st & 4th Argent a chevron sable between three fountains proper (SYKES) 2nd & 3rd Gules three  fleur-de-lis or (MASTERMAN) over all the Badge of Ulster, impaling Argent a lion rampant gules between three pheons sable (EGERTON).
Crests: Dexter, A griffin's head, wings endorsed and gorged with coronet as in the arms of (DUGDALE).  Sinister, an arm embowed habited argent, in the hand proper a scimitar or (STRATFORD).
Mantling: Gules & Argent.
Motto: **'Pestis pegrities patria'**. (Slothfulness is a country's scourge).

For DUGDALE STRATFORD DUGDALE who first married CHARLOTTE (died 1832) daughter of ASSHETON, Viscount CURZON, and, second, MARY ELIZABETH (died 1846) daughter of WILBRAHAM TATTON EGERTON widow of Sir MARK MASTERMAN SYKES 3rd Bt. (died 1836).

The House of Egerton is one of the most ancient and distinguished in Cheshire, the 7th Baronet was created Earl of Winton. (From Debrett's Peerage).

This hatchment was erected by Mary Elizabeth Dugdale in memory of her second husband Dugdale Stratford Dugdale. It is unusual as it attempts to show the arms of husband and wife, both of whom were married twice.

**M39** <u>Alabaster tomb-chest</u>. (c.1440). This tomb has not been positively identified, and all records of it have now been lost. It has often been assumed to be in memory of JOHN HANDEWELL, a former Reeve (Magistrate) of Coventry, and his wife ALICE. This is now considered to be incorrect. The error arose because the Handewell inscription in a north aisle window, which Dugdale recorded in 1656, mentions an alabaster tomb. See <u>Note on Dating</u> in the description of window **n111**. There is only one alabaster tomb in the church, so the assumption was that **M39** is Handewell.

The only monuments which Dugdale recorded are the window and the Ferrers brass **M9**,  so perhaps that is all that there were to see. [1]  The Jesse window and the Ferrers effigy (**M18**) had been buried at the beginning of the Civil War. A reasonable explanation is that in 1656 **M39**, on the assumption that it was a member of the Founder's family,  was still in the conventual church.[2] Perhaps the Handewell tomb originally  'in the north aisle', had not survived the years,  particularly the century of neglect since the Dissolution. In any case the existing tomb certainly looks much more like a knight than a chief magistrate. There is a ground plan of the church drawn by John Buckler in 1820 which shows a 'Monument of male and female effigies – Ferrers' in the south aisle. Apart from identifying the monument it also shows that the organ had not yet been placed in its present position. It also shows the rood screen in its previous place, to the east of the chancel arch.

It is now assumed that **M39** is one of the Ferrers, perhaps that of WILLIAM, Lord FERRERS of Chartley, and his wife ELIZABETH BELKNAP daughter of Sir Adam Belknap,  or EDMUND, Lord FERRERS  of Chartley, and his wife Elene.[3] It is of no significance that both this monument and the Ferrers brass, have a panache of feathers on the helmets. A panache of feathers was not particularly associated with the Ferrers as they were in general use prior to the adoption of crests.[4]

The 'knight' is shown lying with his wife on his right, with his head resting on a tilting helmet, the crest of which is a plume or panache of feathers. He wears a pointed bascinet, ridged in front, encircled by a wreath of which the divisions are alternatively plain and ornamented by a leaf. There is an ornamental band either side of the face opening, carried to the back on the shoulders. The body is covered by the steel gorget and breast-plate with placcate; the latter is plain on the edge, the upper point fits underneath the edge of the gorget. There is an eye on the placcate which fits through a slit in the gorget and is secured by means of a pin. The épaulières are of three pieces. The pallettes over the armpits are shield-shaped. The steel covering of the arms and legs have an ornamental band at the seams. The elbow-pieces are plain with a simple lobe covering the inside joint above and below there are a pair of stiffening plates. The hands, above the gauntlets, are together in the attitude of prayer, but the details are not visible, the fingers having been broken away. Part of the thumbs show that they were laminated steel plate. There is a skirt of seven taces with an ornamental baudric over the fifth; the dagger was attached to this but has broken away. The sword has also gone; it was supported from a narrow diagonal sword-belt, which passes over the baudric. There are tuilles, apparently continuous all round the hips, the side ones are rather larger than the front pair. The knee-caps are globular, with a pair of short stiffeners above and below; they are equal in size, and there is, over the shins, a long extra plate as well. The feet are covered in pointed sollerets; they rest against a lion,[5] which symbolises bravery.

His wife is shown on her husband's right, her head resting on two tasselled pillows, with watching angels, one on each side. She wears a netted horned head-dress, with three pearls at each intersection of the net. This is partially covered by a veil which hangs down behind. There is no wimple, and her kirkle is cut low at the neck. Round her throat is a double chain from which is suspended a cross. She wears a very short and tight-fitting cote, over a kirtle with tight sleeves and pleated skirt; this is long and entirely covers the feet. These rest against two small dogs with long drooping ears and bell collars; they are playing with her skirt. The dogs are a symbol of fidelity. From her shoulders hangs a long mantle secured by a cord which passes through a large square brooch on each side, and hangs below the knees with tassel ends. The side of the tomb-chest is enriched by five angels, each holding a shield, standing between small buttresses; over each in the moulded string is a carved four-leaved flower.

A very similar monument, for Sir Hugh Willoughby and his wife – 1445, can be seen at Willoughby-in-the-Wolds, Nottinghamshire. It is possible that both tomb-chests were made in Nottingham. The angels on the front at Merevale are characteristic of the Chellaston type.[6] For further details of the Chellaston alabaster quarries see Note on Monuments which precedes the descriptions.

1    Dugdale 1656, p 783.
2    Wilson 1934, 5 October 1943
3    Callwood 1985-90, p 25.
4    Woodcock, T.,  Norroy and Ulster King of Arms, personal communication 27 May 1997
5    Chatwin 1921, p 59.
6    Chatwin 1921, p 81.

**M40**    Ornate Cartouche. **'In memory of JOHN STRATFORD DUGDALE, K.C. second son of W.S.DUGDALE Esq., born July 30th 1835 died October 27th 1920. Recorder of the City of Birmingham 1877-1920. Chairman of Quarter Sessions of this County 1883-1920. First Chairman of Warwickshire County Council 1889-1919. Member of Parliament for the Nuneaton Division 1886-1892. Chancellor of this diocese. He married ALICE daughter of H.A.Carleton, C.B. In the course of a long life of service to this county he endeared himself to his many friends in all classes, by his natural courtesy and unselfishness. The righteous shall be held in lasting remembrance'.**

**M41** <u>Framed Photograph</u>. ' **The Chapel of St John, Bentley, 1837-1971**'.

**M42** <u>Hatchment</u>. Sinister background black. Qly, DUGDALE and STRATFORD, impaling CURZON.
Motto: **'Resurgam'** (I shall rise). Cherubs head above shield.
For CHARLOTTE daughter of ASSHETON, Viscount CURZON, first wife of DUGDALE STRATFORD DUGDALE. She died 30th December 1832.

# APPENDIX A

Biographical Notes: Matthew Holbeche Bloxam, Antiquary, 1809-1888
Henry Clutton, Architect, 1818-1893

<u>Matthew Holbeche Bloxam</u>, F. S. A., (1809-1888)

Matthew Holbeche Bloxam was born at Rugby in 1809, and was educated at the school, where his father was one of the masters.

After leaving school he was articled to a lawyer in Rugby, and his early duties – to search the registers of country churches – took him to many of the old villages of Warwickshire and the neighbouring counties, and formed the environment by which his early tastes were moulded and the work of his life slowly matured. He began to make sketches of monuments and porches, fonts, windows, and crosses, and then to study and compare his observations. His interest was soon aroused by the remains of British camps and Roman roads, and he devoted all his leisure to the study of all ancient remains, long before their value and interest were generally understood. In 1829 he published a small volume, *The Principles of Gothic Architecture.*

In 1844 an important work began to appear; it is generally known as *The Churches of Warwickshire,* for that was its original intention. Actually it only consists of churches in the Deanery of Warwick. The historical side was written by the Rev. William Staunton and the descriptions of the architecture of the churches and the monuments were by Bloxam. It was issued in parts, the 12th part in 1857 being the last, owing to the death of the Rev. Staunton. Bloxam's contribution greatly increased the authority, accuracy, and value of the work. He also had a large share in the *Memorials of Rugby*, which was illustrated by C. W. Radclyffe. In the *Brasses of Northamptonshire*, by the late Franklin Hudson, ninety brasses were described by Bloxam from his rubbings and notes. His long life and comparative leisure enabled him to visit many parts of England where Gothic remains were found, and to prepare more than two hundred papers on various subjects to various archaeological societies.[1] He was elected a Fellow of the Society of Antiquaries in 1863, and became the local secretary for Warwickshire.

In June 1864 Bloxam addressed the Leicestershire Architectural and Archaeological Society on *Merevale Abbey.* Also in the same month he talked to the Archaeological Institute at Warwick on *Some Rare and Curious Sepulchral Monuments in Warwickshire in the Thirteenth and Fourteenth Centuries.* Both papers were later published.

In his paper *Merevale Abbey* Bloxam includes an interesting anecdote which had been published in *Literary and Miscellaneous Memoirs* by Joseph Craddock in 1828. Craddock had married Anna Stratford, third daughter of Francis Stratford, and in about 1768 he stayed for a few months at Merevale Hall. Whilst there, he was asked by Lord Leicester, a descendant of the Ferrers, to try and locate the tomb of the

Founder of the Abbey. With the clerk, the sexton, a crow-bar and a spade, and feeling he said like Friar Lawrence, they made some attempt at digging but soon thought the better of it. During his stay he visited Richard Geast, his brother-in-law, at Blythe Hall, which he describes at some length.[2]

Nearly all his life was passed in Rugby, and he naturally felt a great interest in the school. He died on 24th April, 1888, in his eighty-third year, and was buried in a spot that he had chosen, at Brownsover, not far from Rugby, 'near the site of an ancient British fortress'.[3]

[1]    Chatwin 1959,  p 4.
[2]    Craddock vol 1 1828, pp 21-28.
[3]    Timmins 1886, p 131-3.


<u>Henry Clutton</u>  (1819-1893)

Henry Clutton of 76 Onslow Gardens, South Kensington, was born in London in March 1819 and died in West Drayton in 1893. He was distantly related to the Cluttons, Chartered Surveyors, of 5 Great College Street, London. After the death of his father in 1834, his guardians articled him to Edward Blore, the well-known architect. At the completion of his articles Clutton appears to have been Blore's representative during the final stages of the building of Merevale Hall. Blore had first visited Merevale in April 1838 to meet the owner, whose intentions were merely to add some bedrooms to the old house over the existing dining-room. He found that the walls were not strong enough and the plan was abandoned in favour of 'a handsome and very comfortable design' in Blore's confident Jacobean and Elizabethan style. The new Hall took five years to build. Drawings at the Hall show that Clutton worked at Merevale under Blore prior to April 1844 when Blore made his last visit. The remaining work at the Hall – the moving of the front door etc. – was carried out by Clutton. They had co-operated earlier on a design for restoring Merevale Church, including a tower and spire, a gatehouse and lodge, which is dated 1840, when Clutton was only twenty-one.  Clutton designed Baddesley Church, the foundation stone of which was laid by Mr Dugdale in August 1845. In 1849 he made a partial excavation of some of the foundations of the conventual church (published in *The Ecclesiologist* Vol X 1850, pp. 304-313), and in 1848-9 he designed the Gatehouse, which was originally intended as a parsonage, and  the archway. Blore's idea for the archway had been for a classical building with a pediment, pilasters and a tower, but Clutton characteristically decided on an intensely medieval gatehouse.[1] It was based on the Gatehouse at Whalley Abbey which he knew well.

In 1850 Clutton restored the Church of Our Lady, building vestries on the demolished nave side aisles. He also inserted the remains of the Jesse window that had been buried and found at Merevale Hall c.1820 in the east window.[2]

Henry Clutton's work for Dugdale was an important step in his career and gave him, through Dugdale's friends, further commissions. In Dugdale's social circle godparents, gamekeepers, and architects were exchanged with the confidence that came from personal experience. In March 1850 Dugdale paid Clutton 'the balance for building the parsonage, gatehouse, churchyard wall. It has cost more than I expected – not far short of £4,000. I have done with building,' (Diary 29th March, 1850).

In 1856 Clutton and William Burges won the first prize in a competition for work at Lille Cathedral, and although they received the prize money their design was never used.  Clutton believed it was because he was not a Roman Catholic. In the same year he submitted a scheme for the restoration of the Chapter House at Salisbury Cathedral. It met with approval, but having told the Dean that he shortly intended applying for admission to the Church of Rome, he failed to get the contract for that work as well.

In 1860 he married the daughter of an Anglican vicar, who had become a Catholic, George Dudley Ryder, whose brother-in-law was Henry Manning, later to become Archbishop of Westminster and a Cardinal. He paid the price for secession in the way of social ostracism and, initially, the loss of clients. Even the promise of being the architect of the proposed new Westminster Cathedral came to nothing. All the secular works he carried out between 1846 and 1883 were for members of the Protestant community. He more or less retired at an early age due to his failing eyesight. He estate was valued at £98,000.[3]

One gets the impression that in his career he was frustrated and disappointed, and perhaps his happiest times were his earlier days when he was working for Mr Dugdale at Merevale on the various projects.

1    Hunting 1979.
2    Welsh 1973, p x
3    as above, p vi


## Other Clutton buildings in the Midlands.

– Hoar Cross Hall, Hoar Cross, Staffordshire, for Mr Hugo Meynell  Ingram. Neo-Jacobean style. 1862-71.
– Moorhouse Chapel, Moorhouse, Nottinghamshire, for Viscount Ossington, of Ossington Hall. Vigorous 12thC French Gothic style.1860-61.
– St Nicholas Church, Baddesley Ensor, for Mr W.Dugdale. 1845-48.
– St Peter's Church (RC), Leamington Spa. A noble building. 1861-65.
– St Mary's Church, Dunstall, Staffordshire, for John Hardy, of  Dunstall Hall. 1852-3. Also the School and Rectory.
– The Theological School (RC), Hagley Road, Birmingham. Italian Renaissance style. 1860-64.
– Welcombe, Stratford-upon-Avon, for Mr Phillips. Cost £35,000. 1861.
– Widmerpool Hall, Nottinghamshire, for Major Robinson. Sumptuous neo-Elizabethan style.1872-3.

# APPENDIX B

## LIST OF ABBOTS OF MEREVALE ABBEY
and
## INCUMBENTS OF THE CHURCH OF OUR LADY

Notes: In some cases the date may be approximate.
These names also appear in the INDEX

## ABBOTS

WILLIAM, died 1192
REGINALD, elected 1192, resigned 1194
HENRY, Sub-Prior, elected 1194
WILLIAM, occurs 1285
JOHN, elected 1294
THOMAS, occurs 1421
JOHN RIGGELEY, occurs 1450 and 1458
JOHN FREEMAN, 1463
JOHN, occurs 1497
JOHN BADDESLEY, occurs 1517 and 1518
WILLIAM ARNOLD, occurs 1525-1538

## INCUMBENTS

1665-1687  –  Peter MOUSHALL
1754  –  William BIDDLE
1772  –  Christopher PRESTON
1773  –  Moses COTTERELL
1774  –  Arthur MILLER
1780  –  Robert HARRINGTON
1795  –  Thomas CLARE
1816  –  Charles G. OKEOVER
1826  –  W. BRADLEY
1847  –  Thomas JACKSON
1852  –  F. H. LASCELLES
1856  –  B. ASTLEY

|  |  |
|------|------|
| 1872 | Hugh BACON |
| 1906 | Frank TIBBETTS, Curate |
| 1907 | Conrad HOWLAND |
| 1911 | P. R. HUMPHREYS |
| 1926 | H. R. B. MORGAN |
| 1949 | M. A. GURNEY |
| 1952 | Arthur DUTTON |
| 1956 | H. MORLEY-WELLS |
| 1963 | Frank TODHUNTER |
| 1980 | Peter BUCKLER, Priest-in-Charge |
| 1983 | Stanley MARRIOTT |
| 1986 | Alan CALDWELL |
| 1992 | Derek CARRIVICK |

# APPENDIX C

## Victorian Glass Manufacturers

BURLISON & GRYLLS – Windows **nV** and **s11**

Both John Burlison (1843 – 91) and Thomas John Grylls (1845 – 1913) trained in the studios of Clayton & Bell.  Burlison's father, John Burlison Snr (1810 – 68), was principal assistant to the architect G.G. Scott for over twenty-five years.  In 1868, at the instigation of the architects G. F. Bodley and Thomas Garner, Burlison & Grylls founded a stained glass studio at 23 Newman Street, London.  Garner was apparently responsible  for their initial guidance in stained glass and Bodley trained them as church decorators.  Much of their earliest and best glass was made for G. G. Scott and his son G. G. Scott, Jnr.  Thomas Henry Grylls (1873 – 1953, known as a Harry Grylls) took control of the firm on the death of his father and became a founder Fellow of the British Society of Master Glass Painters in 1921.  The firm continued in business until 1953.

Other windows

1870  Broughton, St Mary, Oxfordshire.  Chancel south window (for G. G. Scott Jnr).
1873  Hawstead, All Saints, Suffolk.  West window.
1875  Ellesborough, St Peter & Paul, Buckinghamshire.  South aisle easternmost.
1875  Plumtree, St Mary, Nottinghamshire.  East window.
1875  Alstonefield, St Peter, Staffordshire.  East window.
1878  Beulah, Eglwys Oen Duw, Breconshire.   Two chancel windows.
1882  Mirfield, St Mary, Yorkshire.  East window.
1890  Bedworth, All Saints, Warwickshire.  East window (for Bodley).
1899  and later.  Eccleston, St Mary, Lancashire.  Full set of windows (for Bodley).

CLAYTON & BELL – Window **n11**

John Richard Clayton (1827 – 1913) and Alfred Bell (1832 – 95) became partners in 1855 and their studio soon became one of the largest in the Victorian period.  The firm was carried on by John Clement Bell (1860 – 1944) and Reginald Otto Bell (1884 – 1950), and is still  continued by Michael Charles Farrar Bell (b. 1911).

## Other windows

1858   Cattistock, St Peter and St Paul, Dorset.   West window (Jesse Tree).
1859   Rochester Cathedral, Kent.  North transept, upper tier.
1859   Coleshill, St Peter and St Paul, Warwickshire.  East window.
1861   Hollington, St John, Staffordshire.  East window.
1861   Wymering, St Peter and St Paul, Hampshire.  Full set of windows.
1863   Windsor, St George's Chapel, Berkshire.  East window.
1868   Llandysilio, St Tysilio, Montgomeryshire.  East window.
1871   Chorleywood, Christ Church, Hertfordshire.  Three north nave windows.
1879   Cambridge, King's College Chapel.  West window.
1893   Lichfield Cathedral, Staffordshire.  North transept (Jesse Tree).


## WAILES &  STRANG – Window sV1

William Wailes (1808 – 81) established a stained glass business in Newcastle in 1838 which soon became, along with John Hardman & Co., the largest provincial studio in England.  His output was vast (the 1851 census records that Wailes was already employing seventy-six workers), but unfortunately no archives have survived and the identities of his workforce remain obscure.  Two of Wailes's principal designers in the early years were James Sticks and F. W. Oliphant, both of whom came from James Ballantine in Edinburgh, along with John Campbell, William Mein, Henry Sticks and A. J. Sticks.  George Josphen Baguley (1834 – 1915) was a designer for Wailes in the 1850s and 1860s, before setting up his own studio in Newcastle in 1867; this too enjoyed a considerable success.  Wailes's son-in-law, Thomas Rankine Strang (1835 – 99) became a partner in the business in 1861 and as Wailes & Strang the firm continued to make stained glass until c.1914.

## Other windows (the earlier examples, up to 1858, are William Wailes)

1842   Hursley, All Saints, Hampshire.  North aisle east window.
1845   Trent, St Andrew, Dorset. Chancel lateral windows.
1845   Solihull, St Alphege, Warwickshire. East window.
1847   Wigan, All Saints, Lancashire.  East window.
1848   Beechingstoke, St Stephen, Wiltshire.  East window.
1853   *et seq.* Leavesden, All Saints, Hertfordshire.  Complete set of windows.
1854   Macclesfield, Christ Church, Cheshire.  East window (pictorial).
1858   Blymhill, St Mary, Staffordshire.  South aisle west window (Jesse Tree for G. E. Street).
1874   Bildestone, St Mary, Suffolk.  East window (Wailes & Strang).
1912   Setmurthy, St Barnabas, Cumberland.  East window (Wailes & Strang).

WARD & NIXON / WARD & HUGHES – Window **s111** and part of **1**

Thomas Ward (1808 – 70) and James Henry Nixon (1802 – 57) were partners by, at the latest, 1836, when they made the east window of Owston Ferry Church, Lincolnshire. Nixon had worked on the restoration of the fifteenth-century glass at St Neot's, Cornwall, with J. P. Hedgland and Benjamin Baillie in 1829. The partnership between Ward and Nixon broke up *c.* 1850 and Nixon was soon replaced by Henry Hughes (1822 – 83) who became chief designer for the firm. From the mid-1860s Hughes produced windows under his own name as well as for Ward & Hughes. On Hughes's death in 1883 the firm was taken over by a relation, Thomas Figgis Curtis (1845 – 1924); it remained in operation for a few years after Curtis's death under the control of his cousin, Mrs Ethel Kibblewhite.

Other windows

1843  Farningham, St Peter and St Paul, Kent. East window.
1850  Forest Row, Holy Trinity, Sussex. North nave, easternmost window.
1858  Longdon Green, St James, Staffordshire. Chancel windows.
1860  *et seq.* Thorpe Malsor, All Saints, Northamptonshire. East window, and complete set added until 1891. Especially fine is the chancel south window of 1889.
1869  Guildhall Library, City of London. Main window.
1883  Bromsgrove, St John Baptist, Worcesterhsire. North aisle, Henry Hughes memorial.
1888  Bampton, St Patrick, Westmorland. Chancel windows.
1889  Amersham, St Mary, Buckinghamshire. North aisle, 'Virtues' window.

# APPENDIX D

## Nonconformists at Merevale in 1687

In the Bodleian Library there are three letters dated August and September 1687 concerning Nonconformists and Merevale Chucrch. They are reproduced here by kind permission of the Bodleian Library, Oxford – MS. Tanner 29, fol. 59 (Addison, 11 Aug), MS. Tanner 59, fol. 74 (Addison, 3 Sept), and MS. Tanner 131, fol. 223 (Walmisley, 14 Sept).

## Note on Nonconformists and the Act of Uniformity of 1662.

The Act of Uniformity of 1662 was the most important of the laws restoring the Anglican establishment passed by the Cavalier Parliament of Charles II, following the Restoration. It commanded universal adoption of a slightly revised form of the Elizabethan Prayer Book. All ministers had to give their 'unfeigned consent and assent' and take a declaration of loyalty which resulted in the 'Great Ejection' of about 2,000 Presbyterian, Independent and Baptist ministers. This final parting of the ways between Anglicans and Puritans led to the birth of English Nonconformity.

In 1670 the Scottish Parliament passed an Act against Conventicles. This legislation was against field preaching and illegal house services conducted generally by Presbyterian ministers who had been ejected for nonconformity. The punishment for infringing the act was death and conviscation of goods. It was required by everyone, on oath, to give information regarding conventicles, and those who had had their children baptised by nonconforming minister could be exiled. Gilbert Burnet (Bishop of Salisbury) claimed King Charles himself said that bloody laws did no good and he would not have sanctioned the act if he had known of it beforehand. Despite this admission the repressive policy was maintained [1]

## To: The Most Rev. His Grace The Archbishop of Canterbury,
Lichfield. August 11th  1687

May it please your Grace,
    Since I last waited upon your Grace, I have had no small solicitude to keep this city free from Conventicles; which I praise God I have hitherto effected.
    But that which I am chiefly to acquaint your Grace with, is the carriage of

Mr Moushall, Minister of Merryval in Warwickshire, who has, and does, permit Non-Conformists to preach in the parish church of Merrival, by which irregularity the service of the church is excluded, and the whole become conventicle.

I wrote to Mr Moushall (as Archdeacon of Coventry) to remove the abuse, but received in answer that he had promised the Non-Conformists leave to preach there and that he could not go from his word, withal he told my messenger that Merrieval  was not within my jurisdiction but yet was a peculiar belonging to your Grace.  And this I could not but signify to your Grace.

This Moushall by reason of his infirmities of body, hath been proffered the assistance of his neighbouring Divines, but he has refused them, to take in the Non-Conformists.  I shall not, at present, provide your Grace with any account of the buildings (which [indecipherable] all that for them) because I intend to do it very fully by Mr P. [indecipherable] whom I now daily expect.

I am your Grace's most
obedient servant
Lancelot Addison


To: The Most Rev. His Grace the Lord Archbishop of Canterbury.
Lichfield. September 3rd 1687

May it please your Grace,
    Some weeks ago I acquainted your Grace with the irregularity that has been used of late in your Grace's peculiar of Merrival in Warwickshire, but the minister of the place is now dead, and the enclosed (which I received from a worthy Divine, next neighbour to Merrival) will inform your Grace of the affair: so that I would give your Grace no further trouble.

The King was pleased to lodge here at the Deanery, and has taken particular notice of your Grace's building here: The whole Court and Gentry of the Country have also viewed them and all very greatly commend them.  I had all things in very good order and the King left us very well pleased, which is all I have to provide your Grace with at present, besides my humble duty.

I am your Grace's most
obedient servant
Lancelot Addison

To:  Sir Richard Raines,
Judge of the Admiralty and Prerogative Court of Canterbury.
Lichfield. September 14th. 1687

Honoured Sir,
I was from home all the last week; but I have now, both searched the office, and sent to Miravale; and yet cannot make such a discovery, as I would wish, or you may very well expect.  For our records are altogether silent; and the In[ab]itants there know little or nothing about it.  I find in Sir Wm Dugdale's Antiquitys of Warwickshire, that in the Reign of King Stephen, there was a monastery founded at Miravale, and there continued, till the dissolution in Harry the 8; so that I am apt to believe, that the ordinary jurisdiction, was first in the Bishop of the diocese; and when the prior and convent grew wealthy and potent, taken from him and lodge in them.  For so I observe it to have been in all the parallel instances within the diocese; and thence it was, I have so often minded you of getting a com[mission] from his Grace, to visit the Peculiars.  I must confess, I cannot find any jurisdiction exercised in this Peculiar, in the metropoliticall visitations; as I do in almost all the rest, throughout the whole diocese; which looks indeed as though it were one of the King's Free-Chappells;  But the tradition, with us, and thereto, is to the contrary; and upon the account of the monastery, seems very probable.  But this doubt may be solved by a view of the grant of the revenues of this monastery, out of the Crown (the Rectory of the Church, without all peradventure, being parcel thereof). So far as I can learn, Mr Simonds and Mr Stratford, and their progenitors, have time out of mind, been possessed of the Rectory, and from time to time, as vacancies have happened,  by turns, appointed persons to serve the cure of the souls; paying them an annual stipend of 17 pounds for so doing. That the persons so appointed have successively taken possession of the Church and officiated, without any other admission or allowance:  And it seems very likely; For in all such cases (you know Sir) the Patentees, to this day, nominate curates and where the jurisdiction is never  so regularly executed, the Bishop does no more than grant a licence thereupon, ad deserviendeum curae animarum etc.
The Generality of the inhabitants, I perceive, are too inclinable to bring in a nonconformist; and I know Mr Stratford to be of the same stamp:  But the present turn, they say, belongs to Mr Simonds and what he intends, I do not yet understand.  Some report he has committed the choice to a relation he has in Atherston (about a mile distant from Miravale) who is a rigid fannatique.  However, I verily believe they will scarce adventure to introduce an unqualified person (tho' some such, we are told, have lately taken upon them to preach there): For they seem to be very much startled at the Enquiry we have made.  The Church itself (by the form and proportion) seems to be a very ordinary parochial church.

None of the inhabitants remember any official or registrar, or any ecclesiastical jurisdiction exercised amongst them. They have a tradition that before the horrid Rebellion in the Reign of Charles the first, the Lord of the Mannour kept courts, for Probate of wills, etc; and in all probability it may be true, supposing the manor to be part of the Revenue belonging to the monastery. But for this, there is not any [fol.222v] Evidence now extant. Since the restauration, nobody knows of any single instance of any kind of ecclesiasticall jurisdiction, not so much as of any will proved in common form; or of any admonition or licence granted; saving that one matrimonicall licence is found which was granted by the Master of the Facultys.  But thence you know no inference can be made. The notion the Inhabitants have of the Jurisdiction is that it belongs to his Grace; But they have not any reason for it, and therefore I am very confident, it will appear to be, as before guessed by

Sir
Your most obliged,
most obedient humble servant
W. Walmisley

In 1985 the author wrote to the Dean of Lichfield Cathedral, asking for any information or background concerning the letters. The following is the reply that he received from Rev Prebendary E. C. C. Hill.

61, The Leasowe,
Lichfield,
Staffordshire. WS13 7AH. March 30th 1985.
Dear Mr Austin,
    The Dean has passed your interesting letter, concerning Merevale Church, on to me as Librarian.
    With regard to the ecclesiastical jurisdiction I can claim but little knowledge. A 'peculiar' is a parish, living, college or other institution which does not come within the ordinary jurisdiction of the Bishop but has special privileges. Westminster Abbey, for example is a 'Royal Peculiar'.  A powerful religious community might, as the letter suggests, be in the position of being the only controlling authority.  In the case of Merevale the claim was that the Archbishop of Canterbury was the authority, and so Merevale was a peculiar of his.
    Dean Addison accordingly wrote to the Archbishop of Canterbury (William Sancroft 1677 – 1691).  He, besides being Dean, was also Archdeacon of Coventry, and so felt responsible.
    At this time in Lichfield the Bishop's Palace, destroyed in the Civil War, was being rebuilt.  The Bishop of Lichfield (Wood) was a very unsatisfactory bishop and had been suspended.  Hence Archbishop Sancroft was responsible for the

building.    He chose Edward Pierce as architect and delegated the task of organizing the work to Dean Addison. The foundations were laid in May 1686, and the building was completed in October 1867.  This explains the reference in the letter of 3rd. September to "your Grace's building".  The King is James II.

Merevale appears as in the Archdeaconry of Coventry and the Deanery of Arden in Willis' "Survey of Cathedrals" 1727, with  Mr Stratford as Patron and the abbey as the source of the Church.

Yours sincerely,
Eric Hill
(Hon. Librarian)


1    Douglas 1974, p 259.

# APPENDIX  E

## MISCELLANEOUS

1. The Rood Screen
2. The Wall Painting
3. The Box of Glass
4. The Carved Oak Fragment
5. The Floor Tiles
6. The Kneelers
7. The Baxterley Crozier


## 1. The Rood Screen

In the inventory of goods confiscated and sold at the suppression of the monastery on 13th October, 1538, is an item of 'the particion of olde tymber in the body of the churche',  i.e. the rood screen in the nave. It sold for 1s.

What the screen was like is shown by sketches made by John Buckler in 1820, and preserved in the Manuscript Department of the British Museum. They show a structure of two distinct parts and of two different dates.  The earlier was a thirteenth-century stone screen, roughly 18ft. 6ins. long, standing in the chancel arch. This screen was a solid wall except for the fenestration formed by a trefoiled arcade of ten arches, five on either hand of an acutely pointed two-centred doorway in the middle. Immediately to the east stood an oak gallery of fifteenth-century construction, consisting of a centre section and a wing projecting into the south aisle. When it was in the nave of the conventual church there must have been a similar wing attached to the other end. This would have made the whole screen of a length which presumably fitted between the piers in the Abbey nave. The screen and gallery together were taken down some time between 1840 and 1863, and the stone screen done away with. *The Building News* (17 December 1875) has an article on the restoration of the church including the sentence 'There are fragments of a very fine stone screen laying about the churchyard, embedded in the earth and overgrown with weeds and grass'. The south aisle wing was detached and presumably destroyed while the centre section was set up for an organ gallery at the west end of the nave, where it still stands. In the Abbey nave the rood-screen would have been one bay west of the Pulpitum with an altar against its western face, and supporting the great Rood or Crucifix with the attendant figures of the Virgin Mary and St John on either side.

The screen has a richly moulded framework, carried on posts and brackets, its floor having horizontal joists underneath.  It measures 21ft 3ins long and 5ft 2ins

*The Rood Screen, to the east of the chancel arch*
*(John Buckler, 1820)*

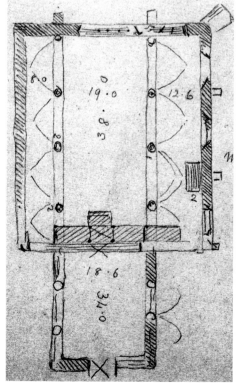

*Plan of the church (John Buckler, 1829) showing*
*the Rood Screen and the Ferrers' alabaster*
*monument **M39** in the chancel*

from front to back.  In the centre is a rectangular projection of 2ft 4ins making a total of 7ft 6ins from east to west.  The projecting part is 6ft 5ins wide. The parapet is subdivided by buttressed stiles into compartments of two panels in each, with tracery in the head.  The middle projection comprises three compartments and each of its return ends two compartments, between four compartments on either hand, with three compartments at each return end, making twenty-one compartments or forty-two panels altogether.  The height of the parapet inside is now 2ft 11ins. but this is not the correct original height, since the floor has been raised above its original level.[1]

[1]    Vallance 1947, p 113.


## 2. The Wall Painting

In the autumn of 1991 the author noticed some  small paint markings on the plaster above the chancel arch. With the help of photography it appeared that there was possibly painting across the whole width of the chancel. In particular there were the heads and up-stretched hands of three praying figures on the south side of the oculus, some drapery folds on the north side, and some red roses above a red line which went across the whole painting.

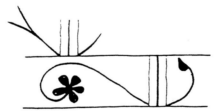

*Reconstruction of masonry pattern c.1250, from the Wall Painting*

*Three Praying figures c.1340, from the Wall Painting*

The photographs were sent to Dr David Park of the Conservation of Wall Painting Department of the Courtauld Institute of Art. His reply (1st November, 1991) included the following:

'Many thanks indeed for the photographs of the Merevale paintings, which are certainly very intriguing. The iconography of the paintings is rather puzzling.  It seems fairly clear that the figures are praying to an image in the oculus (presumably in stained glass?).  Perhaps they are apostles forming part of a Last Judgement, in which case the Majesty would have had to have been represented in the oculus (however, would there have been sufficient room for other figures such as angels blowing the Last Trump or holding Instruments of the Passion?), and other elements such as the Resurrection of the Dead would have been represented lower on the wall.  Or were the figures praying to e.g. an image of the Virgin? (and how would they have related to the rood?).  It is also interesting that the upper part of the wall is simply decorated with scrollwork and rosettes; since the roof is later, is there any possibility of painting at this level?

At first sight they looked c.1320-30, e.g. on the basis of the hands turned up sharply at the wrists.  However, I see Pevsner assigns the chancel arch to the late 13th century, and I cannot see any compelling reason why they should not be this early – the 'broad fold' draperies and other aspects of the style would fit a late 13th- or early 14th century date.  Since the Hailes *capella* paintings are datable to c.1320-30 or slightly earlier, and a recently discovered Crucifixion wall painting at Forde also to c.1320, it is therefore quite possible that the Merevale paintings are the earliest surviving Cistercian figure paintings in England!  I would be very interested in your thoughts on the dating of the chancel arch and oculus (and on how the  latter functioned)'.

In January 1992 Dr Park came to Merevale and made an inspection with a ladder. He found that there were two phases of painting. Underneath is a red masonry pattern of c.1300 and painted over it in parts a figurative design of not later than c.1330-40. He confirmed that the latter was amongst the earliest Cistercian figure paintings in England, and were of national importance. He recommended that a wall painting conservator be asked to make a thorough examination from scaffolding, and to provide a condition report and an estimate for conservation work. In the event John Burbidge, of Granville & Burbidge, came in March 1992 and gave a report and quotation.

A copy of the report is available for inspection in the Church, and it should be consulted for details. The area of the painting is max. height 3.28m, max. width 6.15m. In the centre is the oculus, diameter 1.14m., with a rebate for glazing on the nave side. The report confirms that the upper half contains various masonry designs c.1240 and the lower half has a figurative scheme c.1340. This ties in precisely with the building of the church, floor tiles of 1240 and post 1340, and later the refurbishments and the erection of the south aisle around 1340. The iconography is unknown but it may have included stained glass of the Virgin Mary in the oculus. The condition is poor with much flaking plaster and it is in urgent need of restoration. There are extensive fillings from a previous restoration which has not helped very much.

The report ends with the following proposals -

'These important wall paintings are in urgent need of conservation. Much could be done to stabilise them and improve their legibility. The fragmentary nature of the superimposed schemes will no doubt still cause them to be visually confusing after treatment. However we recommend that it is conserved in situ. In order to improve the display we recommend the installation of a low voltage lighting system with U. V. filters. It would also be worthwhile to consider creating a small exhibition with suitable text, good quality photographic reproductions and possibly diagrammatic reconstructions.

The conservation of this fragile and damaged wall painting is a matter of some urgency.'

Since 1992 it has come to light that in the Tristram Archive at the Courtauld Institute there is a brief note which states 'Above the chancel arch there is a round window between chancel and nave. On the east side there is a scroll pattern in red and white round this window. There are also some faint signs of wall painting over the chancel arch'. Either Professor Tristram or one of his assistants presumably came to Merevale in the 1920s or 1930s.

## 3. The Box of Glass

In 1991 a wooden box, 28"x26"x6", of medieval stained glass was found in the basement of Merevale Hall. On the lid was written in chalk – "CHURCH GLASS FROM MEREVALE – FRAGMENTS OF OLD PIECES OF STAINED GLASS FROM MEREVALE CHURCH". It contained over 450 pieces packed in sand, some of which however were fragments. Search had been made to find the stained glass which had been taken out of the top lights in **n111** and **n1V** some time after 1947.

*Pieces from the Box of Glass*

These had been described in the V. C. H. and elsewhere – see the notes on windows **n111** and **nIV**. However none of the missing glass was in the box. What was in it was glass that must have been taken out of the church when some of the five nineteenth century windows were inserted. In date they ranged from fourteenth century grisaille to sixteenth century Flemish work. Many of the pieces are related to similar glass still in the church and these are mentioned in the text on the various windows.

Amongst the identifiable pieces were ~ the Virgin Mary ~ St Stephen the Protomartyr ~ St Christopher ~ the Christ Child ~ a roundel of Jonah being fed to the whale ~ an Old Testament battle scene ~ the Prodigal Son ~ a greyhound from Deveraux armorial bearings in **n1V**~ pieces of the canopy and designs in **n111** ~ tracery of a miniature window as at Stanford-on-Avon (see illustrations) The author photographed 320 pieces, and the RCHME also took copies of over 120 pieces for the National Monuments Record Centre  (Negative nos. BB93/5029,31,33,35,37, 39,41,43,45,47).


## 4. The Carved Oak Fragment

In 1967 a large farm building was erected in the vicinity of the conventual church on the site of the Abbey. In digging some of the stanchion holes the foundations of the nave piers were located. During this work a carved oak fragment was uncovered. The find was handed to  Charles Clarke of Nuneaton, who was on site, and  who was 'watching' the operation on behalf of John Hurst of English Heritage Historic Buildings and Monuments Commission for England. The piece of wood, which was 19inches high and 10inches wide, consisted of a crested design with formalised fronds. (See illustration, drawn by John Hurst)

Mr Hurst took the carving to Nuneaton Art Gallery and Museum where it was cleaned, and where it has remained on temporary loan and in safe-keeping until it was decided where to place it permanently.[1] Research has been done by Clive Wainwright, Department of Furniture and Interior Design, the Victoria and Albert Museum, who considers it may be part of a screen or the choir stalls, and certainly not part of any domestic furniture.[2] Stuart E. Rigold, Inspector of Ancient Monuments, wrote a description of the piece as follows -

'CARVED TIMBER FRAGMENT FROM MEREVALE ABBEY. This is not a structural member but a piece of applied ornament, thistle-shaped in elevation and originally flat at the back.  It was sawn out of a log of oak, not removed by splitting, since the structural centre of the wood is eccentric, but not marginal, to the piece, but has since split away at the back along natural lines of cleavage.  Across the widest part is a shaped chase to fit over a moulded horizontal member, perhaps not quite as simple as the chase might imply, but with a chamfer-and-fillet mould as repeated on the piece itself.  Towards the waist of the piece are two holes for face-pegs to secure it to a flat vertical surface above the horizontal moulding, and the

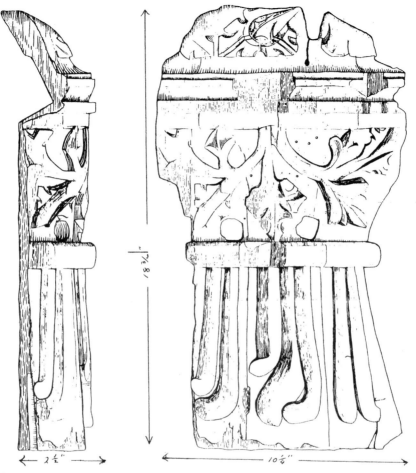

*Carved Oak Fragment*

flat top of the piece itself has two peg-holes, presumably to secure it to a flat horizontal surface, a tester of the underside of a cornice, that overran the whole. One peg remains, with a knobbed head, which would suggest that the horizontal surface was of thin boarding. The over-shadowed cresting that this implies is unusual, perhaps more proper to furniture – a bed or cupboard – rather than to screen-work or panelling. Above and below the chamfer-and-fillet mould are two zones of schematised foliage a rough version of the most usual variety of Perpendicular foliage-ornament, particularly in the Midlands and Marches, with leaves of squarish outline, split diagonally on 'square-flower' principle, and the ribs roughly incised. This is more typical of the earlier part of fifteenth century. It was freely used and much better executed, on the destroyed stalls of St Michael's Cathedral, Coventry. Above the upper zone, at the waist of the piece, is a rough roll, and above this even more schematic fronds that might be interpreted as representing a tuft-like crest of plumes'.

Taking everything into consideration this rare survival from the fittings of the conventual church, dating from around 1430, would seem to be perhaps part of the choir stalls or a screen. It bears no relationship to the rood screen which is already in the nave of Merevale church, and Mrs C. Downes, Archivist of Coventry Cathedral, says that it is unrelated to the destroyed choir screens which were much later, c.1500.[3] Maybe it was part of the decoration on the pulpitum screen.

As a result of negotiations between the author and Gina Quant, Curator of Nuneaton Museum and Art Gallery, and with the help of Sir William Dugdale, the Rector and the PCC, the oak fragment will shortly be returning to the Church of Our Lady. It should also be mentioned that without the help and knowledge of Mr Clarke, who now lives in Weston-Super-Mare, all this would never have happened. Having been stored in a basement of the Museum for thirty-one years, not on public view, it is most satisfactory that it should now be properly exhibited in the church, where it can be appreciated and understood as part of our heritage.

1    Charles Clarke, personal communication 26 November 1984
2    Clive Wainwright, personal communication 2 April 1985.
3    Connie Downes, personal communication 23 October 1997.

## 5. The Floor Tiles

The nineteenth century tiles around the altar are possibly by Minton Hollins of Stoke-on-Trent, and were most likely to have been laid down during the restoration of 1890-3.

There are thirteen medieval floor tiles at Merevale of two groups clearly distinguished by their size. There are six tiles which are larger, c.130mm square, generally known as 'Nottingham' tiles. These are from a well known and very widespread series of fourteenth-century tiles spread across the Midland counties of England, and even up as far as York. In date they are after 1340 and prior to 1400. The other, smaller group, are c.100mm square and are earlier, mid or late thirteenth century. There are seven of the smaller tiles at Merevale.

The reference numbers are from *The Medieval Floor Tiles of Leicestershire* by Norma Whitcomb, Leicester, 1956.

Immediately to the south of the Ferrers' brass (**M9**) there is a row of Nottingham tiles as follows, starting at the east end of the row.

40          80          100          49          24

*The Floor Tiles*

No. 40 – Arms of Ferrers, gules, seven mascles voided or.
> Shield placed diagonally with two leaves either side; quadrant of a circle above it enclosing a small flower.
>
> There are fragments of this design at Bradgate House, All Saints Church, Leicester, and Ulverscroft Priory Museum.

No. 80 – Part of a four-tile design, in entirety a quatrefoil band ornamented with dots and containing four pairs of birds. A pendant from each cusp of the quatrefoil divides the birds.
> There is a similar tile in Leicester Abbey and at Ulverscroft.

No. 100 – Repeating design of a lozenge enclosing a circle within which is an eight petalled rosette. At the corners are quadrants of a circle each enclosing a small eight petalled rosette. Small three-lobed motifs fill the corners of the lozenge.
> Examples are at Croxton Abbey, Leicester Abbey and Ulverscroft.

No. 40 – Another example of the one above, but the upper part of the field is left dark.

No. 49 –  Possibly arms of Gray (armorial bearings in stained glass were recorded in the church in 1656). Barry of six, or and azure.
> Shield placed diagonally; an eight petalled rosette above and one on either side; indented border round edge.
>
> Examples at Croxton Abbey and Ulverscroft.

No. 24 – Arms of England after 1340, quarterly, 1st and 4th gules, three lions passant guardant or, 2nd and 3rd azure, semée-de-lis or. Reversed.
> The shield is placed diagonally with a three-lobed motif either side and a small quatrefoil above.
>
> In 1340 Edward III formally laid claim to France and adopted the style and arms of the Kings of France, which he quartered with the lions of England. They are known as *Quarterly France Ancient and England*.
>
> There is an example at Kegworth Church, amongst many other places.

Of the seven pre-1300 smaller, 100mm, tiles four of them are of a fleur-de-lys design (No. 151). One is immediately to the west of the Ferrers' brass, two are in the centre aisle and one is at the western end of the north aisle. There is an unprovenanced example of this design in Leicester Museum. There are two more tiles in this group in the north aisle and one near the altar steps but these have not been identified. These were all possibly made locally.[1]

In the British Museum there is only one tile from Merevale. It is a fragment from the Duke of Rutland's collection, late fifteenth century, showing the Ferrers' coat of arms (Catalogue reference 278). Elizabeth Eames' *Catalogue of Medieval Lead-glazed Earthenware Tiles*,1980, states that the British Museum's collection contains very few tiles from Warwickshire, other than those at Maxstoke Priory.

In 1969, when the Carved Oak Fragment was found on the site of the conventual church, a quantity of medieval floor tiles were also discovered. They were sent down to the British Museum for identification. The Museum still have them in the basement, stored in six boxes, waiting for someone from Merevale to collect them. At the time of writing (January 1998) the Museum says that, in all probability, the Church of Our Lady could have them back as they are not part of their own collection.[2] Some of them are fragments, but it would be fascinating if they were returned to Merevale and displayed in a manner befitting their historic interest and value.

1    Dr Christopher Norton, personal communication 29 April 1992.
2    Beverley Nenk, B.M., personal communication 29 January 1998.

## 6. The Kneelers

The Merevale Kneeler Scheme was started by Mrs Joan Marriott in the autumn of 1986. The first two that she made were the Wedding Kneelers – Agnus Dei, and Dove with olive branch. By December 1986 twenty-four kneelers were finished, and the Rev. Stanley Marriott conducted a dedication ceremony.

Kneelers have been worked by the following people. The choice of subject and colours has been left to the individual.

John Austin – King Jehosophat from the Jesse Window
Baxterley Eight O'Clock Club – In Memory of Denise Twigg
Jill Chapman – Cross and Crown of Thorns
Jill Carter – Flowers of the Seasons, assisted by her mother Mrs Jennings, her daughters Megan and Beth, and Anna Charles-Jones. (4 kneelers)
Janet and John Cormack, Bibby Cormack – In Memory of Richard and
                                        Marjorie Morgan (2 kneelers)
Fuschia Cormack – The Bell
Janet Cormack – Cockerel
Joyce Cox – Christianity as the Driving Force of the World
        "        – Altar Kneeler
        "        – Halley's Comet
        "        – Stained Glass
        "        – Harvest Festival
David Cox – Merevale Hall
Joyce and David Cox – Kneeling Child
        "                – Steam Carriage

Mrs Day – Cross
Chris Hargreaves – Cat
Jill Hargreaves – In Memory of Dorothy Hudson
　　　"　　　　　– Crosses
　　　"　　　　　– Puffin
　　　"　　　　　– Owls
　　　"　　　　　– Christianity
　　　"　　　　　– Crosses
　　　"　　　　　– Stained Glass
　　　"　　　　　– Village in Summer
　　　"　　　　　– Village in Winter
　　　"　　　　　– The Church Mouse
　　　"　　　　　– Knight in Armour
Edith and Dorothy Hudson – In Memory of Thomas and Mary Hudson,
　　　　　　(Two kneelers)
　　　"　　　　　– Gothic (Two kneelers)
Jane Huntley – The Durham Kneeler
Neil and William Jones – Winter at Merevale
　　　"　　　　　– Summer at Merevale
Jane Knight – Altar Kneeler
　　　"　　　　　– The Dove
　　　"　　　　　– The Ears of Corn
Joan Marriott – Cross Fleurée
　　　"　　　　　– Agnus Dei
　　　"　　　　　– Dove with olive branch
Stephanie Parker – Village in Spring
Ann Prosser – The Cross
Eunice Roberts – Jesus Saviour of men
Keith Roberts – Fishes
Keith Roberts, jnr – Cross
Ruth Taylor – Altar Kneeler
　　　"　　　　　– Village in Autumn
Georgina Trivett – Harvest
Yvonne Trivett – Flowers
Betty Stevenson – Liverpool
Joyce Stewart – We praise You O God
Sunday School – In 1990 a kneeler was worked by children, parents and
　　　　　helpers of the group led by Rosemary Bennett
Joyce Wathes – White Rose

## 7. The Baxterley Crozier

There is a Cistercian artefact in Baxterley Church which is so unusual and interesting that no apology is made for including it here. It is the head of a Crozier from a statue, almost certainly Cistercian, which perhaps commemorated a Saint or Abbot. Baxterley Church, which oddly enough has no dedicatee, was built between 1150 and 1200 and the Crozier head dates from then. The church was one of *ecclesiae nostrae* of Merevale Abbey.

In the winter of 1958 the Chancel arch of the church had to be rebuilt. A brass plaque gives the details. "A Wooden Crozier Head which was part of a Statue, almost certainly Cistercian and of the twelfth century, carved and gilded with details painted in black. THIS CROZIER HEAD was found together with one bone of a young person and another of a sheep when the chancel arch was rebuilt in 1958 after disintegration caused by mining subsidence. These objects had probably been immured in the jamb of this arch during the course of building the church in the 12th/13th century, in accordance with the very ancient custom of thus seeking to imbue a building with strength and stability. The cost of rebuilding the arch in 1958 was borne by the National Coal Board". The items were found in the centre of the wall behind the pulpit. The bones were reburied within the wall and the Crozier Head is in a glass case above the plaque.

This ritual of 'arch burial' was yet another pagan custom taken over by the early Christian church. In this case perhaps a holy relic from a statue at Merevale Abbey was walled-up in the new church to give it sanctity and security. Could one go further and wonder if the statue was that of St Bernard, to whom perhaps the church was once dedicated?

The Rev. H. Morley Wells (Vicar of Merevale 1956-1963) instigated the research, with the help of the Archdeacon of Aston, Birmingham City Museum and Art Gallery, the British Museum Department of Research Laboratory, the Victoria and Albert Museum and the Royal College of Surgeons, amongst others.

# APPENDIX F

<u>The Library at Merevale Abbey</u>.

The medieval books that are associated with Merevale Abbey can be divided into four categories.

<u>Part One</u>

There are five manuscripts in existence that are known to have been in the library at the abbey from the evidence of an *ex libris* inscription, or a note of gift. In medieval times the practice of marking ownership by means of a formal inscription seems to have been widespread in England only in the late-twelfth century and in the thirteenth century, and then only in Cistercian and Augustinian houses. Inscriptions often consist simply of the word *Liber*, the name of the patron saint in the genitive case and the place name in the genitive case, for example *Liber sancte Marie Mirevallis*.

They are as follows -

<u>Cambridge University Library</u> (Ref. Add. 3097) – *Statua – Book of Statutes*, including the legal treatise known as Hengham Parva. It is written in Latin and Law French in a cursive 'anglicana' hand. It was conferred, or given, to the Library by a monk at the abbey, Edmundus de Brantyngthorp (ordained subdeacon in 1349). 14th Century. The MS belonged to Dr John Campbell and was sold by Baker & Leigh on 11 May 1776, lot 27. Later it belonged to Thomas Bateman of Middleton, Derbyshire and was lot 1787 in his sale at Sotheby's 25 May 1893, when it was acquired by Cambridge University Library through Quaritch.[1]

<u>British Museum</u> (Ref. Add. 31826) – *Statua – Book of Statutes*. 13th-14th Century.

<u>British Museum</u> (Ref. Harley 324) – *Breton* (in French). First half 14th Century.

<u>All Souls College, Oxford</u> (Ref. 33) – *W. Malmesburiensis*. Second half 12th. Century.

<u>Winchester College</u> (Ref. 6) – *Josephus*. 12th Century.[2]

<u>Part Two</u>

There is another book known to have survived until the nineteenth century, but it has not been traced since it was offered in the J.S.Hawkin's sale by Fletchers, 8 May 1843, lot 2640. It was *Vitae sanctorum*. 14th Century.[3]

Part Three

There follow details of the forty-one titles that were recorded as being at Merevale Abbey early in the fourteenth century.

In about 1320, a number of Oxford Franciscans journeyed through England, Scotland and Wales and compiled a union catalogue of books on the basis of on-site surveys. It is called the *Registrum Anglie de Libris Doctorum et Auctorum Veterum – England's Register of Books of the Doctors and Ancient Authors*.[4] The *Registrum* starts with a list of 185 monastic and cathedral libraries, which it was intended to visit and which are assigned reference numbers. The catalogue itself lists the titles of roughly 1400 works, attributed to ninety-nine ancient, patristic and early medieval authors. Each title is listed with the references as to where these works were found. Although the list proved to be over ambitious, the friars in the event did visit and record information at ninety religious houses. The *Registrum* is the sole witness to the contents of forty medieval monastic and cathedral libraries, and it preserves the major part of the surviving information about another fifteen.

The Franciscan friars visited Merevale Abbey and reported finding the forty-one titles listed below. Obviously they are only a small part of the whole library. For instance there are no bibles, psalters or service books and nine titles are of a single volume from a set – book 6 etc.It is very difficult indeed to guess the total number of books at Merevale, but if an estimate had to be made, perhaps between 150 to 200 titles might not be far wrong. It is impossible to explain why only forty-one were listed. Perhaps the friars were in some way selective or maybe lists have been lost. Perhaps the friars also purposely failed to list the obvious works. These may have included:

Stephen of Sawley (d.1252) in his *Speculum novitii – The Initiate's Mirror* lists the books that a Cistercian monk or novice should study and which, therefore, any Cistercian library should contain. They are (1) the *Liber usuum – Book of Services*, (2) an *Antiphonarium*, (3) *Vitras patrum – Lives of the Fathers*, (4) the *Dialogi – Dialogues of Gregory the Great*, (5) the *Regula S. Benedicti – Rule of St Benedict*, (6) certain of Augustine's *Enarrationes in Psalmos – Commentary/Narration on the Psalms*, (7) the same author's *Confessiones*, (8) Gilbert of Hoyland's sermons on the Song of Songs, (9) Cassian's *Collationes – Sermons*, (10) certain of Jerome's letters, (11) *Scripta Aelredi – Works of St Ailred* , and (12) William of Saint-Thierry's *Epistola ad fratres de Monti Dei – Letter to the Brethren of God's Mount*.[5] Only one of these 'essential reading' volumes were recorded as being in the Merevale library.

The subject is complicated by these limited resources. In fact only three actual library catalogues from Cistercian houses, those of Flaxley, Meaux, and Rievaulx, have survived. Of the 1,400 titles in the *Registrum* only 360 manuscripts have been traced to all the Cistercian houses where there is any record, though this is fewer than in the library at Meaux Abbey alone.

In a sense however the lack of anything like completeness is secondary to the main and important point about these forty-one titles at Merevale. The historian, after going back in time, through dry and impersonal historical facts and events, through arid architectural reconstructions and suppositions, arrives suddenly face to face, or rather mind to mind, with the monks themselves. With these forty-one books we know something of what they actually read and the language in which they read it, what they thought about and what they discussed. With these forty-one books we are, in a way, as near as we possibly can be to those who lived and worshipped at the Abbey, to their theology, and to the very cause of their existence.

1. The titles of the books, in Latin, are followed in most cases by the first words of the first sentence. Translations are by Dr Ben Benedikz of Birmingham University.
2. The number of each title is the reference in the edition of the *Registrum* edited by Richard and Mary Rouse, Corpus of British Medieval Library Catalogues, The British Museum, 1991.
3. Copies of the titles marked * were also listed in the *Registrum* as being in the library at Bordesley Abbey, the mother house.
4. Comments on, and quotations from the books, and  brief biographical details have been added where possible, mostly from *The Oxford Dictionary of the Christian Church*. 6

## Aelred,

39.7 *De inclusis – Concerning hermits (De institutione inclusarum – Of the principles of hermits)*

St Ailred (1109-1167), Abbot of Rievaulx. He was present at the canonisation of Edward the Confessor in Westminster Abbey and later wrote of his life and miracles. He wrote a prose eulogy of St Cuthbert  and a number of treatises of the Christian faith and life from a mystical  viewpoint. He became known as 'the English St Bernard'.

## Alexander Nequam,

42.7 *Regule super theologiam – Rules of theology* (a rewrite by Alan of Lille)
A MSS. of this work was formerly at Ripley Castle, Yorkshire.

## Augustine, St of Hippo,

1.9 *De libero arbitrio  lib.3 – Concerning free judgement Book 3. Dic michi queso te utrum – Tell me, I beg you,—*.

1.13 *De vera religione lib.1 – Concerning true religion Book 1.Cum omnis uite bone ac beate – A good and blessed life —*. *

1.120  *Responsa Augustini ad consulta Orosii – Augustine replies to Orosius. Licet mutiac probamtissimi – The most approved (person) —*.

1.200  *Dialogus – Dialogues.*

1.272  *De mirabilis mundi – Concerning the miracles of the world.* (unidentified)

1.305 *Sermo super Mulierem fortem – Sermon on the Virtuous Women. Prestabit nobis Dominus – May the Lord be with —.* A sermon on Proverbs, xxxi: 1-31.

Augustine (354-430). Bishop of Hippo Regius in Numidia in Roman North Africa, and greatest of the Latin Fathers. His voluminous writings massively influenced Western thought in later centuries. In many conflicts, including the Reformation, both sides claimed his patronage, appealing to facets of his ever-shifting mind. He died as Roman Africa succumbed to the Vandals, besieging Hippo.

Bede,

7.4  *De schematibus et tropis – Concerning schemes and tropes* (embellishments in the mass).

A book on the methods of writing Latin

7.7  *Super Thobiam – On Tobias.*

7.27  *Exposiciones ex ortographia – Exposition on spelling. Eternus, etas, equitas – Eternal, states, justice.*

St Bede (c.673-735). Biblical scholar and 'Father of English Church History'. His extensive Biblical commentaries were highly esteemed by his contemporaries and immediate successors. Less than a century after his death he was honoured by the title of Venerable. His earliest works, one of which is 7.27 above, appear to have been written for the pupils of the monasteries.

Bernard, St Abbot of Clairvaux,

34.21  *Super Cantica Canticoram lib.1 – On the Song of Songs book 1. Vobis fratres alia quam – You brethren, others than —.*

As might be expected, the entry in the *Registrum* contains an above-average number of reports of St Bernard titles from Cistercian houses, although this is the only one at Merevale.

St Bernard (1090-1153) was one of the most influential religious figures in Europe. He was largely instrumental in establishing the Cistercian Order.

Caesarius,

20.2  *Exhortaciones ad monachos – Sermons to the monastic brotherhood.* *

St Caesarius (470-542). Archbishop of Arles from 502 and a prominent administrator in southern Gaul. He was a celebrated teacher.

Cassiodorus,

14.4  *Super Cantica Canticoram – On the Song of Songs. Osculetur me – Let him kiss me —.** (the opening words of the Song of Songs).

Senator Cassiodorus Flavius Magnus Aurelius (c.485-c.580). He was a Roman author and monk, founding two monasteries on Benedictine lines. One of these he made into a kind of academy and encouraged secular and religious learning and the copying of MSS, and thereby established the monastic tradition of scholarship that preserved the classical culture of Europe during the Dark Ages.

## Cyprian,

21.5 *De Dominica oracione – Concerning the Lord's Prayer.*

   21.7  *Quantum prosint elemosine – How much are alms — ?*

St Cyprian (d.258). Bishop of Carthage. His writings, mainly short treatises and letters, have always been popular, and are valuable sources for ecclesiastical history as well as being sometimes of theological importance.

## Gilbert of Hoyland,

56.9  *Super Cantica Canticoram – On the Song of Songs.**

Listed under 'Opera Gilberti', but presumed to be by Gilbert of Hoyland from the number of Cistercian houses of which copies of this work were recorded, ie Ford, Woburn, Buildwas, Rufford, as well as Bordesley.

This is the only specific title in Stephen of Sawley's list – see (8) above – that is recorded as being at Merevale. It was written as a continuation of St Bernard's Commentary 34.21 above.

## Gilbert of Poitiers,

56.3  *Super Psalteriun – On the Psalter.*

Gilbert (1076-1154). Scholastic theologian. Bishop of Poitiers from 1142.

## Gregory, St Pope, the Great,

2.11  *Speculum eius – His Mirror.*

A tenth-century collection of extracts from Gregory's *Moralium super Iob lib – Moral Instruction on the Book of Job* by Adalbert of Metz.

Gregory I, St (540-604). Pope from 590, the last of the traditional Latin 'Doctors of the Church'. Apart from his achievements of administration, he was a fertile author. He made important changes to the liturgy and fostered the development of music.

## Hugh of St Victor,

97.3  *Super illud – On the same. Tota pulcra es – Thou art all favour —.*

97.4  *De archa Noe lib 5 – Concerning Noah's ark book 5. Priam itaque demonstrandum est – Therefore can be demonstrated —. **

97.15 *De clericali disciplina – Concerning clerical discipline. Quia largiente Domino – Through the most generous Lord —**

97.16  *Super Lamentaciones Ieremie lib.1 – On the Lamentations of Jeremiah. Quomodo sedet – How doth the city sit —.*(the opening words of the Book of Lamentations)

97.17  *De sacramentis lib.2 – concerning sacraments book 2. Arduum profecto – **

97.18  *De operius trium dierum lib.1 – Concerning the works of three days. Inuisbilia Dei – The invisible things of God —* *

97.19  *Didasacolion lib.6 – The Teacher's Book 6. Omnium expetendorum – All eagerness —*\*

Hugh (d.1142). Theologian. In 1115 he entered St Victor, an Augustinian house of canons, in Paris. He wrote on grammar, geometry and philosophy.

## Innocent,

30.2  *Tractatus de missa – Treatise of the Mass* *

## Jerome,

6.73  *Super Danielem lib.1 – On the Book of Daniel book 1.*\*

6.76  *Super Matheum lib.4 – On St Matthew's Gospel.*\*

St Jerome (342-420). Biblical scholar. Spent 4-5 years as a hermit in the Syrian desert, where he learnt Hebrew. His greatest achievement was translating most of the Bible into Latin. He wrote many Biblical commentaries. His passionate nature lead him into many controversies

## Origen,

10.24  *Super librum Numeri omelie 28 – On the Book of Numbers Homily 28. Divin is numeris non omnes –* *

Latin translation by Rufinus. Origen also wrote homilies on many other books of the Old Testament, some of which were translated by Jerome. These Latin homilies were widely read in medieval monasteries and have a rich manuscript tradition.

Origen (Origenes Adamantius) born c.188 probably in Alexandria – died c.254 in Tyre, Phoenicia. He was probably the most important theological and biblical scholar of the early Greek Church. His greatest work is the *Hexapla,* which is a synopsis of six versions of the Old Testament. Jerome said that Origen was the greatest teacher of the early church after the Apostles.

## Peter of Blois,

46.2 *Super Iob belligeronticon* (a corruption of *Basiligeronticon – for the ageing king*)

The beginning of the prologue reads *Incipit Basiligeronticon, id est ludus H(eurici) Senioris regis.*

## Peter of Poitiers,

59.1  *Super Boicium de Trinitate – On Boethius concerning the Trinity.*

59.2  *De hebdomadibus – Concerning the seven days.*

Listed as this but these works are not by him. It is perhaps a copying mistake. The two titles were probably together in a codex at Merevale and are probably by Boethius. This would then resemble a similar title now in the Bodlein Library.

The most famous work of Boethius (c.480-c.524) was *De Consolatione Philosophiae*, in five books, and written in prison. It concerned philosophies leading the soul to God, and was ground for debating whether he was a Christian. This was answered affirmatively in his *De Trinite*.

Rabanus,
   11.10 *Super Genesium – On the Book of Genesis.*
   11.17 *Super Leuiticum – On the Book of Leviticus.*
   11.18 *Super Numeri – On the Book of Numbers.*
   11.19 *Super Deuteronomium – On the Book of Deuteronomy*
Rabanus Maurus (776-856), theologian, master of the monastery school at Fulda Abbey in Hesse, which under him became one of the most influential in Europe. He wrote a manual for the clergy and Biblical commentaries. He was a prolific poet and the *Veni Creator Spiritus – Come, Holy Ghost, our soul*s *inspire* has often been attributed to him. It has been used at Vespers at Whitsuntide since the tenth century.

Richard of St Victor,
   98.17 *De Beniamyn et fratibus eius – Concerning Benjamin and his brothers.* *
Richard (d. 1173). He was at the Augustinian house of canons, St Victor, in Paris.

Robert of Cricklade,
   54.3 *De Connubio Iacob – Concerning the marriage of Jacob.* *
Surviving copies include one from Cirencester now in Hereford Cathedral, and one from Reading now in the Bodleian.
   There was a Hospice at Cricklade.

Robert (of Tumbalena ?),
   54.11 *Super cantica canticoram – On the song of songs.*

Seneca,
   83.11 *Epistole ad Lucillium – Letter to Lucillius.*
Seneca's (b. 4 B.C.) character was despicable. His work is included as an example of excellent and exemplary Latin prose, and was used as a style textbook.

Part Four

In the Bodleian Library there is an early fourteenth-century manuscript *The Rydware Cartulary*. It is a register of all the estates and possessions of Sir Thomas Rydware in Staffordshire, Leicestershire and Warwickshire. In the Introduction of a modern transcription edited by George Wrottesley, it states that it was probably compiled by a monk at Merevale[7]. The manuscript contains some contemporary marginalia of which the illustration is an example. It is typical of the witty *drolleries* or *grotesques* of the period.

*Marginalia from The Rydeware Cartulary*

1   Ringrose, J.S., Librarian, Cambridge University Library, personal communication 15 January 1986.
2   Ker 1964, p 130.
3   Ker 1987, p 49.
4   Rouse 1991.
5   Bell 1992, p xxiv.
6   Livingstone 1987.
7   Wrottesley 1895, p229

# APPENDIX G

### Dugdale's 'Merevale' and The Inventory

1. Copy of Dugdale's entry 'Merevale' in his *Antiquities of Warwickshire,* 1656.
2. Copy of the the Inventory of the Abbey taken at the Dissolution in 1538.

## 1. Copy of Dugdale's entry 'Merevale' in his *Antiquities of Warwickshire,* 1656.

The following is copied  from the first edition. Dugdale's footnotes have been omitted. The diagrams of 1656 show twenty–one coats of arms in the stained glass, to which the 1730 edition has an added  note – 'Most of these are gone or broke'. Two Latin inscriptions are also given in the first edition which are both now lost. The one on the Ferrers brass is included in the description of the monument **M9,** and that on the Handewell monument in the description of window **n111**. There are useful additional footnotes and other information in the 1730 edition (edited by Dr William Thomas) which are not present in the later 1765 edition, and which make it the most useful.

"Westwards from **Atherstone**, scarce a mile, stands **Merevale**, of which there is no particular mention in the Conquerour's Survey, in regard it was involved with **Grendon** (lying on the other side the River) whereto it then belonged as an Out–wood, and therewith became possessed by Henry de Ferrers, a great man in these parts (as I shall show anon) whose grandson Robert Earl Ferrers, having a reverend esteem of the Cistercian Monks, which in his time began to multiply in **England**, made choice of this moutainous and woody Desert (as fittest for solitude and devotion) to found therein a Monastery of that Order; which was begun accordingly in the xiith year of King Stephen's reign; and being propagated with Monks from **Bordesley** Abbey in **Worcestershire**, had, by reason of such its situation, the name Merevale attributed thereto; the lands wherewith he endowed it, being these; viz all his Forest of **Arden** (id est his Out–wood in that part of the Woodland, which then bore the name of **Arden**) and also what he had in **Whittington**, together with the Manor of **Overton** (now called **Orton** on the HIll in Com. Leicestershire) as also **Herdivike** in the **Peake** of **Derbyshire**, unto **Cranokeloune**; with Common of pasture in **Hertenbon** and **Pillesburie**, for Sheep and other Cattell, as the words of his Charter do import.

But besides this, it had several other Benefactors; of which the principle were these, Gerard de Limest, Walt. de Camvile, Raphe de Baskervile, and Pain de Baskervile, as K.H. 2 Charter, whereby he ratified their grants, manifesteth: So that about 30 H.2 there were the Granges of **Moze** (now **Moze–Barne**) **Bronz Seile**, little **Peatling**, the Church of **Overton** (on the Hill) with the Chapells of **Grendon**, **Livicrosse**, **Copthall** and **Baxterley** (some in this County, and some in

**Leicestershire**) belonging thereto, as the Bull of Pope Lucius the third, whereby he confirmed them, doth manifest. Diverse lands had these Monks afterwards bestowed on them also, through the bounty of sundry other persons; viz in Little **Sheyle** by Henry de Appelby and others; In **Overton** subt. **Arden** by John de Overton and Rob. Stapleton. In **Brantingthorpe** by Rob de Brantingthop and others; In **Sheepy** by Nick de Temple and others. In **Hertyndon**, as parcel of the Manor of **Pillesbury**, they obtained Cxx. acres of land more, from Thomas Earl of **Lancaster**, in lieu of xxs, yearly Rent, which they usually did receive at his Exchequor of **Tutbury**.

In 2 E.3, they had a grant of two Messuages, three Shops, and xiis, Rent in **Leicester** by Petronill Oliver of **Leicester**, to find a Priest for celebration of Divine service in the Conventual Church Of **Merevale**, for the soul of her the said Petronill, her ancestors and all the faithful deceased. In 11 E.3 they had more lands bestowed on them, lying in **Overton**, **Peatling**, and **Brantingthorpe** before specified, by sundry persons. In 18 E.3 they purchased xvii Messuages, and diverse lands in **Atherstone**, **Bentley**, and **Baxterley**, with the moytie of the Manor of **Baxterley**. In 31 E.3 they had a Messuage and a yard land in **Bentley**, bestowed on them by John de L'isle, then Lord of the Manor, to find xv. Tapers in the Chapel of Our Lady, near the Gate of the Abbey. In 10 R.2 they purchased six other Messuages in **Atherstone**, and certain Rents in **Whittington** and **Baxterley**. In 16 R.2 four Messuages and certain lands in **Tamworth** and **Wilnecote**, as also to Messuages more in **Atherstone**. And in 28 H.6 they obtained the Church of **Mancetter**, with an appropriation thereof. The value of all which lands and all other their possessions, amounting until CCLiiii l. i s. viii d. as appears by the Survey of 26 H.8 preserved it from ruin, when the lesser houses went to wrack in 27 H.8. But in 30 H.8 it was overwhelmed in the general deluge being surrendered to the King's use, by the then Abbot and Covent, as their public instrument, under the Conventional Seal, dated 13 October the same year, whereunto their names are particularly subscribed, doth manifest; whose pensions during life, as they were by Patent granted to them, I have here also added.

Willielmus Arnold, Abbas, xl 1.
Joh. Ownsbe, Sub–Prior, v l.vi s. viii d.
Edm. Bromley, alias Crockell, v l. vi s. viii d.
Will. Tunman, v l. vi s. viii d.
Rob. Fenne, v l.
Thomas Benson v l.
Will. Robynson, Sacrista vl. vi s. viii d.
Joh. Dunne, v l. vi s. viii d
Wil. Bron, v l.
Joh. Spey, Liii s. iiiid.

After which, viz, 2. Dec. 32 H.8 was the site hereof, with the lands and woods adjacent, together with  **New–House**–Grange, and **Pinwell**–Grange, in Com. Leicestershire.  As also **Owisthirn**–Grange in this Countie, granted to Sir Walt. Devereux Kt. Lord Ferrers of **Chartley**, and to the heirs male of his body; so that there being a reversion in the Crown, for defect of issue male, in 4 E.6 he obtained another Patent (being then arrived to the dignity of Viscount of **Hereford**) for the same site, and the other lands, to himself and his heirs generally.  Which Walter disposed thereof to Sir Will. Devereux Kt. his younger son, as it seems; for he it was that patched up some part of the ruins here, and resided thereon, as I have heard.  And by his Testament bequeathing it to Joan his wife for life, gave the remainder to Walter Viscount **Hereford** (his nephew) and his heirs; Which, Walter (afterwards created Earl of **Essex**) left issue Robert Earl of **Essex**, attained in 43 Eliz.   Whose son and heir Robert being restored, now ( anno 1640) possesseth the site thereof, and much of the lands".[1]

*Merevale Abbey: Note the Gate Chapel bottom left. (Painting by P. A. Baker, Conjectural design by the author, 1996)*

## 2. Copy of the Inventory of the Abbey, taken at the Dissolution in 1538.

This Inventory was recorded in the *Book of Inventories* in the Court of Augmentation Office 1541–2. It was printed in Latin in Dugdale's *Monasticon Anglicanum*, 1655–1673, and in English in an edition of 1817–1830. The spelling has here been modernised, and explanatory words and comments have been added in brackets.

"Hereafter follow the names of all and every such person and persons as were by Thomas Leigh, doctor in law, and William Cavendish, auditor, commissioners appointed by the King our Sovereign Lord, for the Dissolution of the Monasteries, following by them indifferently chosen and sworn of, and for the valueing, rating, and apprising of all and singular the goods and cattle coming and being found at the surrenders, taken in the same late dissolved Monasteries and Priories within sundry shires or counties the names as well of the said houses as of the persons so sworn following hereunder written in order.

That is to say:

### MERYVALE

| | | |
|---|---|---|
| Robert Greene | Raffe | John Blunt |
| William Swyft | Rye. Hytson | Henry Coke |
| John Ramson | Xpofer Dryaton | John Abell |
| William Hogekyns | William Rop | Edmnd Stokton |

The late Monastery of Merivale in the County of Warwickshire.

Hereafter follows all such parcels of implements or house–hold stuff, corn, cattle, ornaments, of the church and such other like found within the late Monasterie there at the time of the Dissolution of the same house sold by the King's Commissions to the Right Honorable Lord Ferrers as particularly and plainly follows.

That is to say:

| **The Church** | £. | s. | d. |
|---|---|---|---|
| First, a table of alablaster | 0 | 5 | 0 |
| Item, 2 candelsticks of brass | 0 | 5 | 0 |
| Item, one lamp of latten (an alloy similar to brass) | 0 | 0 | 8 |
| Item, the monks seats of timber | 0 | 1 | 0 |
| Item, a pair of organs | | | |
| (portative organs – see window **sV**) | 1 | 0 | 0 |
| Item, 6 old altars with images (carved figures) | 0 | 2 | 0 |
| Item, the partition of old timber in the body of the church (the Rood Screen – see Appendix E) | 0 | 1 | 0 |
| Item, 3 iron candlesticks before the altars | 0 | 1 | 0 |
| Item, a holy–water stoup of brass | 0 | 1 | 0 |

| | | | |
|---|---|---|---|
| Item, the glass and the iron in the windows of the church | 2 | 0 | 0 |
| Item, all the pavement in the church | 0 | 10 | 0 |
| Item, 6 grave–stones with brass in them (perhaps these include monuments **M5**, **M6** and **M26**) | 0 | 5 | 0 |
| | 4 | 11 | 8 |

**The Vestry**

| | | | |
|---|---|---|---|
| Item, 4 old single tynacles of countfeit bawdkyn (a tunicle is a vestment resembling the dalmatic, worn by subdeacons over the alb at the Eucharist. These were of richly embroidered cloth with imitation silver and gold thread) | 0 | 4 | 0 |
| Item, a suit (chasable, dalmatics etc of the same colour and materiel) of old red taffeta, painted. | 0 | 1 | 8 |
| Item, a suit of old purple taffeta | 0 | 1 | 0 |
| Item, 2. tynacles of tawney taffeta | 0 | 1 | 4 |
| Item, a suit of crimson velvet, and a cope suiteable to the same | 2 | 13 | 4 |
| Item, a suit of white bawdkyn lacking the vestment with a cope to the same | 0 | 15 | 0 |
| Item, 2 copes of red bawdkyn | 0 | 13 | 4 |
| Item, 2 suites of scenett | 0 | 3 | 4 |
| Item, a cope of green satin with a boss of copper on the breast | 0 | 10 | 0 |
| Item, a cope of crimson velvet | 1 | 0 | 0 |
| Item, an altar cloth of old blue damask with images (figures) embroidered | 0 | 3 | 4 |
| Item, certain old altar cloths painted | 0 | 1 | 0 |
| Item, 5 old altar cloths painted and 2 towels | 0 | 0 | 8 |
| | 6 | 9 | 0 |

**The Cloister and the Chapter House**

| | | | |
|---|---|---|---|
| Item, 24 panels of painted glass | 0 | 5 | 0 |
| Item, the paving of the same with the roof timber and slate | 0 | 16 | 8 |
| Item, a laver of ley metall and leade before the same laver (a washbasin of pewter and lead. Remains of the stone surround near the Refectory can be seen) | 2 | 0 | 0 |
| Item, a great dragge of nett there (a drag–net was used to snare birds as well as to catch fish) | 1 | 0 | 0 |
| Item, in the Chapter House three windows of glass | 0 | 3 | 0 |
| | 4 | 14 | 8 |

**The Hall** (The Refectory)

Item, 3 tables and 7 formes.  Item, 2 cupboards      0     3     4

**The Buttery**

Item, 2 ambries (large food cupboards)

Item, 8 plain table cloths   Item, 3 towels

Item, 5 tubs for ale.  Item, a piece of leade in the intre

    (waste pipe?)      0     2     0

**The Cheffe Plor** (linen chest?)

Item, an olde counterpane and a coverlet.

Item, 2 blankets and a bolster. Item, a featherbed

    and a mattress.  Item, a tester (a bed canopy of

    painted cloth) with curtains of dornyxe (a silk/wool

    fabric – from the Flemish town Tournay).

Item, the hanging of old green say (serge).

Item, one old carpet for the table.

Item, 6 cushions.  Item, 2 chairs.  Item, a pair

    of andirons. Item, a table and three forms      1     6     8

**The Inner Chamber**

Item, a featherbed and a bolster.

Item, a coverlet and 1 blanket.  Item, a mattress      0    10     0

**The great old Chamber**

Item, a featherbed and a bolster.

Item, 2 mattresses.  Item, a vonyng lynyd (fine linen –

    literally 'winning')

Item, olde hangings painted.  Item, 3 old chests.

Item, 2 old coverlets and a bolster      0    13     4

**The Chamber next the Old Chamber**

Item, an old table.  Item, a form and 2 old

    cupboards and one painted cloth      0     1     0

**The Chamber called the Bredonnes**

(bredurne was an early provincial form of brethren.

    Possibly this is the room of the brethren – the dorter

    or dormitorium. The dorter was carpeted with straw

    and the beds consisted of straw pallets. The usual

    'bed linen' was a mat, a woollen covering, a woollen

    cloth under the pillow, and the pillow. The monks

    slept in their habit, apart from the outer garment)

Item, 4 featherbeds and a mattress.
Item, 2 bolsters.  Item, a pair of blankets.
Item, a covering.  Item, a tester of blue linen cloth.
Item, a chair and 2 old cupboards.
Item, 2 mattresses.  Item, 2 coverlets 2 pillows.

| | | |
|---|---|---|
| Item, one blanket | 0 | 10 | 0 |

### The White Chamber

Item, 4 featherbeds and a mattress.
Item, 2 counterpanes  Item, 6 coverlets.

| | | |
|---|---|---|
| Item, 5 bolsters | 0 | 10 | 0 |

### The Porter's Chamber with other Servant's beds.

Item, a mattress and a bolster.  Item, a coverlet
and a wynowe shete ( a sheet over an unglazed
window to keep out the cold).  Item, 3 mattresses,

| | | |
|---|---|---|
| 2 bolsters, and 4 coverlets | 0 | 3 | 4 |

### The Kitchen

| | | | |
|---|---|---|---|
| Item, 4 brass pots | 0 | 7 | 0 |
| Item, 4 kettles and a pan | 0 | 5 | 0 |
| Item, 4 spits | 0 | 4 | 0 |
| Item, a pair of iron racks | 0 | 4 | 0 |
| Item, 2 bars of iron to hang pots on | 0 | 2 | 0 |
| Item, 4 pot hooks | 0 | 1 | 0 |
| Item a morter of brass and pestle | 0 | 1 | 0 |
| Item, a possenett of brasse  (a small pot for boiling with a handle aand three feet) | 0 | 1 | 0 |
| Iteme 27 plates *9s.*, 8 saucers    *1s. 4d* 24 dishes  *2s. 4d.*,  3 chargers  *3s* | 0 | 15 | 8 |
| | 2 | 1 | 8 |

### The Larder House

Item, a powdering trough (in which fish was cured
with salt and spice)    Item, a hogshead of verjoyce
(an acid juice of crab apples, or other sour fruit,
used in cooking and for dosing animals)

| | | |
|---|---|---|
| Item, 3 other tubs there | 0 | 2 | 0 |

## The Brewhouse

| | | | |
|---|---|---|---|
| Item, 2 lead pans of brass | 2 | 0 | 0 |
| Item, 2 vats | 0 | 2 | 0 |
| Item, 11 wort vats (made of lead) | 0 | 11 | 0 |
| Item, 2. mash vats | 0 | 3 | 0 |
| | 2 | 16 | 0 |

## The Malte House

| | | | |
|---|---|---|---|
| Item a cistern of lead to steep malt in | 0 | 13 | 5 |
| Item, a  (blank) to drye malt with | 0 | 1 | 0 |
| | 0 | 14 | 4 |

## The Bake House

| | | | |
|---|---|---|---|
| Item, 4 troughs to boult (sift) and to knead in. | | | |
| Item, 4 tubs.    Item, 2 bultying cloths (used for sifting flour and meal) | | | |
| Item, a molding table.    Item, a round table. | | | |
| Item, skip to carry bread in. | 0 | 3 | 4 |

## The Lime House

| | | | |
|---|---|---|---|
| Item, 6 bushel of white salt in a chest | 0 | 3 | 0 |

## Implements of the Barn

| | | | |
|---|---|---|---|
| Item, 6 syves and ij skypps.  Item a busshell (a drinking bowl) | | | |
| Item, a winnowing cloth and a mare to winnow withall | 0 | 2 | 4 |

## Carts and cart ware

| | | | |
|---|---|---|---|
| Item, a wayne and a cart shod with iron *1l.* | | | |
| Item, 5 pair of geres (equipment) for horses *4s.* | | | |
| Item, 4 ox yokes *2s.* | | | |
| Item, 4 temes (trainers?) and a pair of clenges (hooks?) *2s.* | 1 | 7 | 0 |

## The Smithy

| | | | |
|---|---|---|---|
| Item, an anvil *10s.*   Item, 4 pair of tongues *2s.* | | | |
| Item, 3 hammers *1s.*  Item, a pair of bellowy *3s.4d.* | | | |
| Item 2 grindstones *2s.* | 0 | 17 | 4 |

## Grain at the Monastery

| | | | |
|---|---|---|---|
| Item, wheat there lying together l.19 quarters at 5s. 8d. the quarter | 17 | 0 | 0 |
| Item, barley 1.10 quarters at *3s. 4d.* the quarter | 10 | 0 | 0 |
| Item, more whete and rye together 29 quarters | 5 | 0 | 0 |
| Item, 12 quarters of malt in the brew–house | 2 | 0 | 0 |
| Item, myskelen 12 strks (myskelen is mixed grain, especially rye mixed with wheat. A stryke was a bushel measure, from strickle – a wooden bar used to strike grain at the top of the measure) | 0 | 4 | 0 |
| Item wheat 3 stryks | 0 | 2 | 8 |
| Item, pea and barley 2 stryks | 0 | 1 | 0 |
| | 34 | 7 | 8 |

## Grain at the Newhouse Grange

| | | | |
|---|---|---|---|
| (The fourteenth century barn, over 140ft long, is today owned by the Poulson family. The splendid timbers are in their original state, and the barn is still used for its original purpose). | | | |
| Item barley | 6 | 13 | 4 |
| Item, wheat 20 quart. at *6s.8d.* the quart | 6 | 13 | 4 |
| Item, rye 3 quart at *7s.* the quart | 1 | 8 | 0 |
| Item, peas 12 quart at *4s.* the quart | 2 | 8 | 0 |
| | 26 | 9 | 4 |

## Hay in the Monastery

| | | | |
|---|---|---|---|
| Item, hay 50 loads at *3s 4d.* the load | 8 | 6 | 8 |

## Cattle at the Monastery

| | | | |
|---|---|---|---|
| Item, 6 drawing oxen £5. | | | |
| Item, 5 drawing horses £1. 6s. 8d. | | | |
| Item, 6 young swine *6s* | 6 | 12 | 8 |

## Cattle at the Newhouse Grange

| | | | |
|---|---|---|---|
| Item, 9 kine wih a bull *5l.*  Item, 6 drawing oxen *5l.* | | | |
| Item, 5 drawing horses *4l.* Item, 8 swine and a boar *8s.* | 14 | 8 | 0 |

## Sheep at Crouxston in the Peak

(Lord Ferrers' original grant of land to the Abbey
included 'Hardwicke in the Peake of Derbyshire,
unto Cranokestoune' – Dugdale 1656)
Item, at Crouxstonne in the Peak in the tenure
holding of Rycharde Slyght and William Haryson

| | | | |
|---|---|---|---|
| 80 sheep at *1s.8d.* the piece | 6 | 13 | 4 |

## White Plate Sold

Item, 47 ounces of white plate sold whereof
37 ounces at *3s. 4d* the ounce *6l. 15s. 8d.*; and

| | | | |
|---|---|---|---|
| 10 ounces at *3s. 8d* the ounce *1l. 16s. 8d.*; in all | 8 | 12 | 4 |

| | | | |
|---|---|---|---|
| The sum total of all the goods found within the said late Monastery with *8l. 12s. 4d* for whyte plate soulde | £133 | 12 | 2 |

Certain goods or stuff belonging to the said late
Monastery remaining as yet unsold:

## Gilt Plate

First, broken silver of a cross–staff,
2 chalices, one standing piece all gilt, weighing                  132 oz.

## White Plate (silver)

Item, chalice on little salt without a cover
and 20 spoons, weighing                  26 oz.

## Lead

| | £. | s. | d. |
|---|---|---|---|
| Item, there remains in lead, by estimation, 8 fothers (cart–loads), valued at | 32 | 0 | 0 |

## Bells

| | £. | s. | d. |
|---|---|---|---|
| Item, there remains 4 bells valued by estimation at | 30 | 0 | 0 |

(One of the bells now in Mancetter Church is thought
to have come the Abbey at the Dissolution or earlier.
The living was appropriated by the Abbey in 1449
and a Guild established by Abbot John Riggeley in
1458. The bell is the  4th, diameter 3'8", 15 cwt, note F.
The founder was J. Hose or Stephen le Bellgeter of
Leicester c.1350. It has a Latin inscription which reads,
in English, *This Bell Exists in Honour of Holy Mary*).

Md. there remains all the houses and edifices of the site of the said late monastery, the glass, iron in the windows, pavements, and 6 gravestones in the church, the roof slate pavements, and glass in the cloister, and glasse in the chapter house only excepted and sold.

Md. the said honorable Lord Ferrers was put in possession to our Sovereign Lord the King's use of the site the said late monastery, and all the desmesns to it appertaining the 15th, day of October, in the 30th. year of our said Sovereign Lord King Henry the 8th".[2]

1   Dugdale 1656, pp 782–3.
2   Dugdale 1655–73, pp 484–6

# GLOSSARY

of terms used in stained glass, architecture, heraldry and armour.

AKIMBO – with the hands on hips and elbows turned outward.

ARGENT – the armorial metal silver.

BASCINET – a light helmet, shaped like a skull–cap, worn with or without a movable front.

BENDLET – diminutive of BEND, ie narrow.

BENDLET SINISTER – as above but on the right.

BLACK–LETTER – A general description covering various kinds of lettering, or type–faces generally known as Gothic.

BRASSARTS – plate armour for the upper part of the arm.

CAMAIL – a tippet of mail appended to a helmet.

CARTOON – a full–size drawing made for the purpose of transferring a design to a painting or tapestry. Cartoons were an essential part of the process of making stained glass, and were used in painting by the early 15th century. The design was transferred either by pressing heavily along the outlines with a pointed metal implement called a stylus or by rubbing powdered charcoal through a series of pinpricks – a process called 'pouncing'. In the 19th century, proposed designs for frescoes in the Houses of Parliament were parodied in *Punch*; thereafter the word came to mean a parody or humorous drawing.

CHARGE – an armorial bold shape on a shield.

CHIEF – one of the honourable ordinaries. It is placed on the upper part of the shield, and contains a third part of it.

COUTES – the elbow piece in armour.

CRESPINE – the golden net–cap worn by ladies in the 14th and 15th centuries.

CULT – veneration or honouring of a saint expressed in public acts, local or universal, and formally approved by the Pope.

CUISSES – armour for the thighs.

CUSP – projecting point between the FOILS of a Gothic arch.

DIAPER – fabric woven with a small and simple pattern formed by the threads, etc. and filled in with dots and leaf designs.

FESS – a broad horizontal band across the centre of the shield.

FLASHED GLASS – a white glass to which a thin layer of coloured glass is added when the molten glass is blown. The flashing can be abraded or removed by acid to reveal the colour of the base glass. Red or ruby glass is commonly flashed. It is particularly useful for armorial bearings where the scale is small. A development of the early 14thC.

FOIL – lobe formed by the CUSPING (q.v.). TREFOIL, QUARTREFOIL etc., show the number of lobes or leaf shapes to be seen.

FRET – an interlaced armorial design. See **sV1**.

GADLYNGS – the spikes on the knuckles of the gloves of mail.

GENOUILLIERES – mailed coverings for the knees.

GLAZIER'S POSITION MARK – a letter or mark scratched or painted on stained glass to identify the position of a panel in a window, or a stack of glass being fired in the kiln.

GUARDANT – looking out from the shield.

GULES – armorial red.

IN SITU – glass which is in the position for which it was originally made.

JAMBS – armour for the legs.

LIGHTS – architectural term for the divisions of a window between the ????????

LOMBARDIC SCRIPT – type of handwriting common to northern Italian  MSS. from 7thC. to 13thC.

MARTLET – a strange little heraldic bird, similar to a house martin. It is depicted as having tufts of feathers rather than feet.

MORSE – the clasp or fastening of a cope.

MULLION  – a vertical stone shaft  dividing a window into individual lights.

MURREY – an uncommon armorial tincture of a mulberry colour.

OCULUS – a circular opening in a wall.

OR – the armorial metal gold.

PALE – an ordinary consisting of a broad vertical band in the centre of the shield.

PANACHE – the group of feathers on the apex of the helmet.

PASSANT – walking and looking to the left side with three paws on the ground and the left front paw raised.

POT–METAL – coloured glass made by the addition of metallic oxides. It was a Continental monopoly until the late 16thC.

QUARRY – a diagonal or square pane of glass.

QUATREFOIL – see FOIL.

ROUNDEL – a circular pane, often small, consisting of white glass decorated with glass paint, yellow stain and from the later 16thC, with coloured enamels.

SABBATONS – a system of overlapping articulated plates to cover the shoes.

SOLLERETS – the overlapping plates which formed a mailed shoe.

TACES – flexible bands of armour surrounding the hips.

TORTEAUX – a roundel, or disc, of gules. From the Latin torta – a round loaf of bread.

TRACERY – The ornamental intersecting stonework in the upper part of the window.

TYMPANUM – The area between the lintel of a doorway and the arch above it.

TREFOIL – see FOIL

VAIR – one of the two principal furs used in armory. It originates from the fur of a species of squirrel (varus), which was poular in the Middle Ages for the lining of the garments of those not entitled to wear ermine. The animal` was blue–grey on the back and white underneath. By sewing a number of these pelts together, with blue–grey and white alternating, an attractive design was obtained. (No doubt Cinderella's slippers were made of this fur; verre – glass being erroneously translated from the French instead of vair – fur).

VAMBRACE – armour that covered the fore–arm from elbow to wrist.

YELLOW STAIN – A method of turning white glass yellow, by the applications of a solution of silver compound, and then firing it.

# LIST OF REFERENCES AND BIBLIOGRAPHY

Archer, M., Crewe, S. and Cormack, P. – *English Heritage in Stained Glass:Oxford*, T.A.I., 1988.

Aston, M.– *England's Iconoclasts*, O.U.P., 1988.

Attwater, D. – *Dictionary of Saints*, Penguin Books, 1986.

Badger, E.W. – *Monumental Brasses of Warwickshire,* Cornish Brothers, 1895.

Baker, J. – *English Stained Glass*, Thames and Hudson, 1960.

Baker, J. – *English Stained Glass of the Medieval Period* , Thames and Hudson, 1978.

Barnard, F.P. – *Edward IV's French Expedition of 1475. The Leaders and their Badges, being MS.2. M.16. College of Arms,* Clarendon Press, 1925.

Barnes, A. & Renshaw, M. – *The Life and Work  of John  Snetzler*, Scolar Press, 1994.

Bartlett, Benjamin. – *Manduessedum Romanorum, The History and Antiquities of Mancetter and Ansley.* Nichols, 1791.

Baskerville, G. – *English Monks and the Suppression of the Monasteries*, Jonathan Cape, 1972.

Batt, Rev N. G. – *Coloured  Glass  in Preston–on–Stour*, British Archaeological Association, 1876.

Bell, D.A. (ed.) – *The Libraries of the Cistercians, Gilbertines and Premonstratensians,* The British Library, 1992.

Benham, Rev  W. – *Dictionary of Religion*, Cassel, 1891.

Benton, J. A. – *Medieval  Menagerie,  Animals  in  the Art of the Middle Ages*, Abbeville Press, 1992.

Bloxam, M. H. – *On  some Rare and Curious Sepulchral Monuments in Warwickshire, of the Thirteenth and Fourteenth Centuries,* Paper given to The Archaeological Institute at Warwick. 26 June 1864.

Bloxam, M. H. – *Merevale Abbey,* A Paper read to the Leicestershire Architectural and Archaeological Society.  June 1864.

Bible, The: *A Multimedia Experience*, World Library Inc., 1995. CD–ROM.

Bickley, W. B. (translator) – *Monastic and Other Estates in the County of Warwick*, For The Dugdale Society, O.U.P. 1923

Bond, F. – *Dedications and Patron Saints of English Churches*, Humphrey Milford, O.U.P., 1914.

Bond, F. – *Screens and Galleries*, Henry Frowde, O. U. P., 1908.

Bottomley , F – *The Abbey Explorer's Guide,* Kaye & Ward, 1981.

Bowyer, L. – *The Cistercian Heritage*, Mowbray, 1958.

Bradley, J. – *Illuminated Manuscripts*, Brachen Books, 1996.

Brakspear, H. – *Waverley Abbey*, The Surrey Archaeological Society, 1905.

Brown, S. – *Stained Glass. An Illustrated History*. Studio Editions, 1992.

Brown, S. – *The Fourteenth Century Stained Glass of Mandley, BAA Conference Transactions XV, Medieval Arts, Architecture and Archaeology at Hereford*, BAA, 1995.

Brown, S. & O'Connor, D. – *Glass Painters,* British Museum Press, 1991.

Burman, J. – *Old Warwickshire Families and Houses*, Cornish Brothers, 1934.

Burman, P. (ed.) – *Conservation of Wall Paintings – The International Scene*, Council for the Care of Churches, etc. 1979.

Butler, Dom C. – *Benedictine Monachism*, Longmans Green, 1924.

Butler, L. & Given–Wilson, C. – *Medieval Monasteries of Great Britain,* Michael Joseph, 1979.

Callwood, R. – *Proposed Articles for Merevale Magazine,* (typescript) 1985–90.

Clutton, H. – *Discovery of the Remains of Merevale Abbey,* The Ecclesiologist
    Vol X, 1850.

Chatwin, P.B. – *Incidents in the Life of Matthew Holbeche Bloxam,* Dugdale Society Occasional
    Paper No.13, Dugdale Society, 1959.

Chatwin, P.B. – *Monumental Effigies in the County of Warwick,* Transactions of the
    Birmingham Archaeological  Society, vol. 47, 1921.

Cherry, J. (ed.)  *Mythical Beasts*, British Museum Press. 1995.

Cowen, P. – *A Guide to Stained Glass in Britain*, Michael Joseph, 1985.

Cowen, P. – *Rose Windows,* Thames and Hudson, 1990.

Craddock, J. – *Literary and Miscellaneous Memoirs,* 4 vols, Nichols, 1828.

Crewe, S. –  *Stained Glass in England 1180–1540,* R.C.H.M.E., H.M.S.O.,1987.

Delaney, J.L. – *Dictionary of Saints*, Kaye and Ward, 1980.

Dickinson, J.C. – *Monastic Life in Medieval England,* A. & C.Black, 1961.

Dickinson, J.C. – *Furness Abbey – An Archaeological Reconsideration.* Transactions of the
    Cumberland and Westmorland Antiquarian and Archaeological Society. 1967.

Douglas, J.D. – *The New International Dictionary of the Christian Church,* Paternoster Press,
    1974.

Dugdale, Sir W. – *The Antient Usage in Bearing Arms,* Oxford. 1682.

Dugdale, Sir W. – *The Antiquities of Warwickshire,* London, 1656.

Dugdale, Sir W. – *Monasticon Anglicanum,* London, 1655–1673

Dugdale, W.F.S. – *Merevale Abbey & its Past,* Lecture to Atherstone Archaeological Society,
    Tamworth & Atherstone Herald, 1 March 1913.

Dugdale, W.F.S., – *Merevale Church,* Lecture to Atherstone Archaeological Society,
    Atherstone News, 1922.

Dugdale, W.S. – *MS Diary 1822–1871,* (Unpublished – at Merevale Hall)

Eden,F.S. – *Ancient Stained and Painted Glass,* C.U.P., 1933.

Elder, E. R. – *Cistercians in the Late Middle Ages,* Cistercian Publications, Michigan, 1981

Ellis, R. H. – *Monastic Seals in the Public Record Office,* H. M. S. O., 1986.

Elvin, C. L. – *Dictionary of Heraldry,* W. H. Brown, East Dereham, 1889.

Ekwall, E – *The Concise Oxford Dictionary of English Place–Names,* Clarendon Press, 1960.

Evans, J. – *English Art 1307 – 1461,* Clarendon Press, 1949.

Every, G. – *Christian Mythology,* Hamlyn, 1970.

Fairholt, F.W. – *Costume in England, A History of Dress.* George Bell, 1896.

Farmer, D.H. – *The Oxford Dictionary of Saints,* Clarendon Press, 1980.

Fergusson, G. – *Signs and Symbols in Christian Art,* Zwemmer, 1954.

Fergusson, P. – *Architecture of Solitude: Cistercian Abbeys in Twelfth Century England*, Princeton
    University Press. 1984.

Foster, J. – *The Dictionary of Heraldry, with Feudal Coats of Arms and  Pedigrees,* Bracken Books,
    1989.

Fox–Davies, A.C. (ed) – *Fairbairn's Book of Crests,* T.C. & E.C. Jack, Edinburgh,1892.

France, J. – *The Cistercians in Medieval Art,* Sutton, 1989.

Friar, S. – *A New Dictionary of Heraldry*, A. & C. Black, 1987.

Friar, S. – *Heraldry For the Local Historian and Genealogist,* Allen Sutton, 1992.

Ganderton, E.W. and Lafond, J. – *Ludlow Stained and Painted Glass,* Friends of St Lawrence
    Church, Ludlow, 1961.

Gibson, P. – *The Stained and Painted Glass of York Minster,* Jarrold Publishing, 1992.

Gover, J.E.B., Mawer, A. and Stanton, F.M. – *The Place–Names of Warwickshire*, English Place–Name Society, Vol. III, C.U.P., 1936.

Grant, F. J. – *The Manual of Heraldry*, John Grant, Edinburgh, 1929.

Green, A. R. – *The Romsey Painted Wooden Reredos*, Archaeological Journal, vol. xc. 1933.

Graham–Dixon, A. – *A History of British Art*, BBC Books, 1996.

Hall, J. – *Dictionary of Subjects and Symbols in Art*, Icon Editions, Harper and Row, 1979.

Hall, J. – *Dictionary of Subjects and Symbols in Art*, Harper and Row, 1974.

Hallam, E. (ed.) – *Saints: Over 150 Patron Saints for Today*, Weidenfeld and Nicolson, 1994.

Halliwell, J. O. – *A Dictionary of Archaic and Provincial Words, Obsolete Phrases etc, from the Fourteenth Century.* John Russell Smith, 1865.

Hammand, L.A. – *The Ancient Windows of Gt. Malvern Priory Church,* St. Albans, 1947.

Hamper, W. – *The Life, Diary, and Correspondence of Sir William Dugdale Kt.,* Harding Lepard, 1827.

Harris, M. D. – *Some Manors, Churches and Villages of Warwickshire,* Coventry City Guild, 1937.

Harrison, M. – *Victorian Stained Glass,* Barrie and Jenkins, 1980.

Hicks, C. – *Discovering Stained Glass,* Shire Publications Ltd, 1996.

Hill, B. D. – *English Cistercian Monasteries and Their Patrons in the Twelfth Century*, University of Illinois Press, 1968.

Hinnels, J. R.. (ed.) – *Dictionary of Religions,* Penguin Books, 1966.

Hirst, S.M, Walsh, D.A. and Wright, S.M. – *Bordesley Abbey*, 11. B.A.R, 1983.

Hope , W.H.St J. – *The Abbey of St Mary in Furness, Lancashire,* Transactions of the Cumberland & Westmorland Antiquarian & Archaeology Society, 1900.

Hoult, J. – *Dragons, Their History and Symbolism*, Gothic Image, 1987.

Husenbeth, F.C., – *Emblems of Saints,* Norfolk and Norwich Archaeological Society, 1882.

Hunting, Dr P. – *Henry Clutton (1819–1893), A Biography.* Unpublished PhD. thesis, University of London, 1979.

Husbands, T.B. – *The Luminous Image, Painted Glass Roundels in the Lowlands, 1480–1560,* The Metropolitan Museum of Art, N.Y., 1995.

James, M. R. – *Abbeys,* G. W. R., 1925.

Jenkins, H.M. – *Dr Thomas's Edition of Sir William Dugdale's Antiquities of Warwickshire,* Dugdale Soc. Papers No. 3, The Dugdale Society, 1931.

Kelly, The Rev B. (ed.) – *Butler's Lives of the Saints,* Virtue, 1949.

Kelly, S. and Rogers, R. – *Saints Preserve Us,* Robson Books, 1993.

Ker, N. R. (ed.) – *Medieval Libraries of Great Britain,* R. H. S., 1964.

Ker, N. R. (ed.) – *Medieval Libraries etc, Supplement,* R. H. S., 1987.

Knowles, D. – *Bare Ruined Choirs,* C. U. P., 1976.

Knowles, D & Hadcock, R.N. – *Medieval Religious Houses, England and Wales,* London, 1971.

Knowles, J. A. – *John Thornton of Coventry and the East Window of Great Malvern Priory,* The Antiquaries Journal, 1959.

Knowles, J. A. – *Medieval Method of Employing Cartoons for Stained Glass,* Journal of the British Society of Master Glass–Painters, 1925.

Kovachevski, C. – *The Madonna in Western Painting,* K.& M.Publishing, 1991.

Larkworthy, P. – *Clayton and Bell,* The Ecclesiological Society, 1984.

Lee, L., Seddon G., and Stephens, F. – *Stained Glass,* Chartwell Books, 1989.

Livingstone, E. A. (ed.) – *The Concise Oxford Dictionary of the Christian Church*, O. U. P., 1987.

McCann, Dom J. – *Saint Bernard*, Sheed and Ward, 1937.

Macklin, The Rev. H. W. (revised by C. Oman), – *Monumental Brasses*, Allen & Unwin, 1963.

Maddison, F., Styles, D., Wood, A. – *Sir William Dugdale 1605–1686, A List of his Printed Works etc*, L. Edgar Stephens for W. C. C., 1953.

Madley Parish Church, Herefordshire, – *Church Guide*, n.d.

Mairs, The Rev. A .S. – *The Parish and Church of St Peter, Mancetter*, 1982.

Marks, Prof. R. – *Stained Glass in England during the Middle Ages*, Routledge, 1993.

Marshall, G. – *Ancient Glass in Madley Church*, Transactions of The Woolhope Naturalists' Field Club. Hereford, 1927.

Matarasso, P. (trans. & ed.) – *The Cistercian World, Monastic Writings of the Twelfth Century*, Penguin Books, 1993.

Merton, T. – *Three Studies on St Bernard*, Cistercian Publications, Michigan, 1980

Milward, R. – *A Glossary of Household, Farming and Trade Terms from Probate Inventories*, Derbyshire Record Society Occasional Papers, No. 1, 1986.

Moorhouse, G. – *Sun Dancing, A Medieval Vison*, Weidenfeld & Nicolson, 1997

Morris, E. – *Stained and Decorative Glass*, Tiger Books International, 1990.

Nelson, P. – *Ancient Painted Glass in England, 1170–1500*. The Antiquaries Books, Methuen, 1913.

Newton, P. A. – *Schools of English Glass Painting in the Midlands 1275 – 1430*, (unpublished Ph. D. thesis), University of London 1961.

Norris, Rev. H. – *Tamworth Castle, Its Foundation, its History and its Lords*, Smith, Tamworth, 1899.

Norton, C. & Park, D. (eds) – *Cistercian Art and Architecture in the British Isles*, O.U.P., 1986.

Norwich, J.J. (ed.) – *Oxford Illustrated Encyclopedia of the Arts*, O.U.P., 1992

Osborne, J. – *Stained Glass in England*, Allen Sutton, 1993.

Pennington, M.B. (ed.) – *The Cistercian Spirit, A Symposium*, Irish University Press, 1969.

Pevsner, N. – *The Buildings of England, Warwickshire*, and other volumes, Penguin Books, various dates.

Poole, Rev. G.A – *The Stained Glass of Lowick Church, with Remarks on Glass Painting, Old and New*, Architectural Society of the Archdeaconry of Northampton, 1891.

Powicke, F. M. (trans.) – *The Life of Ailred of Rievaulx by Walter Daniel*, Thomas Nelson, 1950.

Price, G. Vernon. – *Valle Crucis Abbey*, Brython Press, Liverpool, 1952.

Puttock, A. – *A Dictionary of Heraldry and Related Subjects*, Gifford, 1970

Pykitt, D. – *R.I.K.L.O. Newsletter*, No. 29, 1986.

Rackham, B. – *The Glass Paintings of Coventry and its Neighbourhood*, The Walpole Society, 1930.

Randall, L.M.C. – *Images in the Margins of Gothic Manuscripts*, University of California Press, 1966

Rahtz, P. & Hirst, S. – *Bordesley Abbey*, B.A.R. 23, 1976.

Rohery, G. C. – *Concise Encyclopedia of Heraldry*, Bracken Books, 1985.

Rouse, H.R. & Rouse, M.A. (Eds) – *Registrum Anglie De Libris Doctorum et Auctorum Veterum*. The British Library, 1991.

St. Augustine's Abbey, The Monks of, – *The Book of Saints*, A. & C, Black, 1989.

St. Joseph, J. K. S. – *Monastic Sites from the Air*, C.U.P., 1952.

Salzman, L. F. (ed.) – *Victoria County History of Warwickshire*, Vols. 11, 111 & 1V, 1945, 1947.

Scholes, P. – *The Oxford Companion to Music*, O.U.P.,1944.

Shrewsbury, J. F. D. – *A History of the Bubonic Plague*, C. U. P., 1971.

Smith, C. J. – *The Heraldry of Warwickshire Parish Churches and Associated Buildings*, Birmingham and Midland Society for Genealogy and Heraldry, 1987.

Sommerfeldt, J. R. – *Studies in Merevale Cistercian History II*, Cistercian Publications, Michigan, 1976.

Spencer, B. –*Pilgrim Souvenirs and Secular Badges*, Salisbury and South Wiltshire Museums, 1990.

Steinberg, S. H. – *Two Portraits of Sir John of Hartshill*, Antiquaries Journal, No. 19, 1939.

Stephen, Sir L. & Lee, Sir S. (Eds) – *The Dictionary of National Biography*, O.U.P., 1964

Storer, J.& H.S., – *Fountains Abbey*, Ripon, c.1830

Summers, P. (ed.) – *Hatchments in Northamptonshire, Warwickshire and Worcestershire*, Phillimore, 1974.

Taylor–Taswell, Rev. – *Whalley Church and Abbey*, Blackburn, 1905.

Timmins, S. – *A History of Warwickshire*, Elliot Stock, 1889.

Tobin, S. – *The Cistercians. Monks and Monasteries of Europe*, The Herbert Press, 1995.

Toulson, S. – *The Celtic Alternative, A Reminder of the Christianity We Lost*, Rider, 1987.

Toy, J. – *The Windows of York Minster, A Guide and Index*, Dean & Chapter of York, 1985.

Tracy, C. – *English Gothic Choir Stalls 1200–1400*, and *1400–1540*. Boyden Press, 2 vols, 1987 and 1990.

Tristram, E. W. – *English Wall Painting of the Fourteenth Century*, Routledge & Kegan Paul, 1955.

Twining, L. – *Symbols and Emblems in Early and Medieval Christian Art*, Murray, 1885.

Vallance, A. – *Greater English Church Screens*, Batsford, 1947.

Watson, A. – *The Early Iconography of the Tree of Jesse*, O.U.P., 1934.

Watts and Windward. – *The History of Atherstone*, H.M.S.O., 1988.

Welsh, Prof. S. – *Henry Clutton (1819–1893), A Biographical Note, and List of His Principal Works*, Typescript, 1973.

Westlake, N.H.J. – *A History of Design in Painted Glass*,

Wheeler–Holohan, V. (revised) – *Boutell's Manual of Heraldry*, Frederick Warne, 1931.

Whitcomb, N. R. – *The Medieval Floor Tiles of Leicestershire*, Leicestershire Archaeological and Historical Society, 1956.

Williams, D. H. – *The Welsh Cistercians*, 2 vols. Caldey Island, Tenby, 1983

Wilson, Elizabeth – *Spots Steeped in History – Merevale Abbey*, Series of Articles in *The Midland Counties Tribune*, 1934. (partly dictated by W.S.F.D).

Woodforde, C. – *English Stained and Painted Glass*, Clarendon Press, 1954.

Woodforde, C. – *English Stained Glass and Glass–Painters in the Fourteenth Century*, British Academy Proceedings, 1939.

Woodforde, C. – *Stained Glass of New College, Oxford*, O.U.P., 1951.

Woodward, J. M. – *History of Bordesley Abbey*, Parker, 1866.

Wright, T. (ed.) – *Suppression of the Monasteries*, Camden Society, 1843.

Wrottesley, G. – *The Rydware Chartulary* from *Collections for a History of Staffordshire*. The William Salt Archaeological Society, Harris, 1895.

Ziegler, P. – *The Black Death*, Collins, Readers Union, 1969.

# NAMES IN THE CHURCHYARD

Notes

1.    The Rector or a church officer should be consulted to locate the position of the graves in the churchyard.
2.    The dates given are either the date of death or dates associated with other names on the gravestone.
3.    Corrected to February 1998.

ALCOTT, James – 1869
ALCOTT, Mary – 1879
ALCOTT, Mary – 1883
ALLSOP, Cyril Frank – 1971
ALLSOP, Kate Irene – 1997
AUSTIN, Elizabeth – 1754
AUSTIN, Elizabeth – 1790
AUSTIN, Ellen – 1794
AUSTIN, Ellin – 1838
AUSTIN, Hannah – 1792
AUSTIN, Joseph – 1783
AUSTIN, Joseph – 1790
AUSTIN, Lucy – 1805
AUSTIN, Thomas – 1765
AUSTIN, Thomas – 1798
AUSTIN, Thomas – 1861
AUSTIN, William – 1752

BAKER, Elizabeth – 1862
BAKER, James – 1865
BAKER, Sarah Anne – 1834
BAKER, William – 1845
BAKER, William – 1896
BARNETT, Annie Mary – 1949
BEADMAN, Ann – 1775
BEADMAN, Thomas – 1785
BENNISON, Muriel – 1997
BINGHAM, Ann – 1814
BINGHAM, William – 1814
BOX, Eli – 1929`
BOX, Levi – 1971
BOX, Mary – 1946
BOX, Nellie – 1970
BRABSON, Emma – 1811
BRABSON, Thomas – 1811
BROWN, Mary – 1895

BROWN, William – 1791
BUDWORTH, James – 1823
BUDWORTH, John – 1829
BUDWORTH, Mary – 1824
BUTLER, George – 1845
BUTLER, Henry – 1841
BUTLER, John – 1833
BUTLER, Joseph – 1853
BUTLER, Sarah – 1878
BUTLER, Thomas – 1872
BUTLER, William – 1835

CHADAWAY, Charles Thomas – 1948
CHADAWAY, Edith Mary – 1951
CHADAWAY, Mary – 1933
CHADAWAY, Mary Georgina – 1965
CHADAWAY, Samuel Charles – 1938
CLARKE, Ernest William – 1959
CLARKE, Phyllis Ann – 1936
CORBETT, John – 1913
CORBETT, Sarah – 1924
CORFIELD, Arthur John – 1959
CORFIELD, Marion Emma – 1954
CORNOCK, Thomas – 1937
COX, Elizabeth  – 1887

DETHICK, John – 1837
DONALD, Doris Mabel  – 1951
DRURY, Alan Michael – 1996
DUGDALE, Alice – 1949
DUGDALE, Alice Frances – 1902
DUGDALE, Major Arthur George – 1932
DUGDALE, Lady Belinda – 1961
DUGDALE, Blanche Elizabeth Campbell – 1964
DUGDALE, Charles John Geast  – 1944

DUGDALE, Edgar Trevelyan Stratford – 1964

DUGDALE, Edith – 1897

DUGDALE, Edith Cecilia – 1948

DUGDALE, Ella – 1897

DUGDALE, Gladys Margaret  – 1977

DUGDALE, Henry – 1897

DUGDALE, Col. Henry Charles Geast – 1911

DUGDALE, Sir John Robert Stratford, K.C.V.O.–1994

DUGDALE, Lucy Violet – 1895

DUGDALE, Margaret, Lady – 1965

DUGDALE, Mary Eliza Cornwallis – 1931

DUGDALE Mary Louisa – 1923

DUGDALE, Sidney – 1899

DUGDALE, William Stratford – 1882

DUGDALE, William Francis Stratford, Bt – 1965

DUGMORE, W. S. – 1848

DUTTON, Elizabeth – (see Faux)

FAUX, Catherine – 1855

FAUX, Charles – 1866

FAUX, Edward – 1879

FAUX, Elizabeth – 1836

FAUX, Elizabeth – 1877

FAUX, Joseph – 1855

FAUX, Luke – 1857

FAUX, Mary – 1821

FAUX, Richard – 1834

FAUX, Robert Wright – 1855

FLOYD, Joseph – 1855

FLOYD, Mary – 1830

FREEMAN, Raymond Harry – 1993

FURLONG, Dorothy Joan – 1996

GARRATT, Charles – 1849

GARRATT, Elizabeth – 1863

GARRATT, Mary Avins – 1911

GARRATT, Sarah Sophia – 1854

GARRATT, William – 1890

GARRATT, William Edward – 1860

GOODRIDGE, Agnes May – 1991

GOODRIDGE, James – 1985

GORRINGE, Peter –1994

HADDON, William – 1875

HALL, Samuel – 1831

HALL, Sidney – 1995

HARDING, Charles – 1858

HEATHCOTE, Edward – 1790

HENTON, Emma – 1886

HENTON, Sarah – 1886

HENTON, William – 1886

HERBERT, Edward, Earl of Powis – 1911

HOWARD, Edward – 1836

HUDSON, Dorothy – 1995

HUDSON, Mary – 1928

HUDSON, Thomas – 1961

JENKINS, George – 1843

JENKINS, Laura – 1938

JENNINGS, Elizabeth – 1869

JENNINGS, Robert – 1874

JOB, Mary – 1870

JOB, Thomas – 1875

KEEN, Hannah – 1865

KEEN, John – 1873

KEEN, Thomas – 1845

KEEN, William  – 1843

KNATCHBULL-HUGESSIN, Norton Reginald –1941

KIRKHAM, Albert – 1974

KIRKHAM, Mary – 1979

LEWIS, Ann  – 1858

LEWIS, Charles – 1890

LEWIS, Joseph – 1866

LEWIS, William – 1863

LLOYD, John – 1853

LLOYD, Rebecca – 1855

LLOYD, Thomas – 1855

MACFARLANE, Alan Grant – 1947

MACFARLANE, Henry – 1943

MACFARLANE, Jane – 1969

MACFARLANE, Mary – 1896

MACFARLANE, Mary Ann – 1920

MACFARLANE, Peter Grant – 1910

MACFARLANE, Richard Grant – 1876

MACFARLANE, Susan – 1939

MACFARLANE, Walter Mace – 1922

MARSHALL, Colin – 1986

MARSHALL, Doris – 1990
MARSHALL, Frederick Leslie – 1997
MAYLING, Elizabeth – 1864
MAYLING, John – 1859
MCDONALD, Ethel Gertrude – 1993
MICHOT, A. M. – 1848
MICHOT, Elizabeth – 1848
MILES, George – 1850
MILES, George – 1850
MILES, Hanna – 1850
MILES, Harriet – 1850
MILES, Joseph – 1850
MINGAY, Admiral James – 1872
MINGAY, Lydia – 1887
MINGAY, May Constance – 1881
MINGAY, William – 1872
MINGAY, Willam George – 1872
MINION, William Edward – 1874
MITCHESON, George Arthur – 1934
MITCHESON, Sarah Bardsley – 1942
MONTGOMERY, Charlotte – 1911
MONTGOMERY, Hugh – 1911
MORGAN, H. R. B. – 1963
MORGAN, John Lancelot – 1926
MORGAN, Marjorie – 1980
MORSE, John – 1867
MORSE, Mary – 1871
MORTON, Aaron – 1795
MORTON, John – 1788
MORTON, Mary – 1801

NEWEY, Margaret – 1993

OLIVER, Ethel Lilian – 1988
OLIVER, Mark William – 1986

PARRY–MITCHELL, Ellen, Bridget – 1929
PARRY–MITCHELL, Henry Digby – 1914
PAYN, Elizabeth – 1800
PAYN, Elizabeth – 1824
PAYN, John – 1783
PAYN, John – 1821
PAYN, William – 1834
POGMORE, Betty – 1865
POGMORE, Godfrey – 1848

POGMORE, Frances – 1900
POGMORE, Frank Herbert – 1882
POGMORE, John – 1882
POGMORE, Sally – 1827

READ, Harry – 1977
RIPLEY, Richard – 1852
RIPLEY, Thomas – 1852
ROWLEY, Ann – 1811
ROWLEY, Samuel – 1811

SCATTERGOOD, Carl – 1989
SLACK, William – 1856
SLATER, Ann – 1994
SMITH, Ann – 1814
SMITH, Arthur – date obliterated
SMITH, John – 1788
SMITH, Helen – 1915
SMITH, Isaac Cope Franke – 1924
SMITH, Lucy – 1950
SMITH, Mary – 1861
SMITH, Sarah Ann – 1923
SMITH, Thomas – 1869
SPENCER, Elizabeth – 1859
SPENCER, Joseph – 1859
STAIEN, Ann – 1833
STAIEN, Elizabeth – 1833
STAIEN, William – 1832
STAIEN, William – 1833

TAYLOR, Emily – 1953
TAYLOR, Evelyn Mary – 1964
TRICKER, Mary Ann – 1950
TRIVETT, John – 1991
TWIGG, Denise Elizabeth – 1989

WEST, Ada – 1914
WEST, Arthur – 1914
WEST, Kathleen – 1914
WHATMAN, James – 1931
WHITMEE, William Charles John – 1936
WILSON, Emma Denise – 1991
WINDRIDGE, Ann – 1859
WINDRIDGE, Allen – 1859
WOND, Emma – 1950

# GENERAL INDEX

1. Included are all the names on, and associated with, the memorials and monuments in the church, the Incumbents and Abbots, also the names of people connected with the church or Abbey in any way, and mentioned in the book.
2. Some minor references of places are omitted.
3. The names in the Chuchyard are listed immediately prior to this section.
4. Dates are included after names if needed for identification.

Having started this book with a quotation from T. S. Eliot's *Little Gidding*, it would seem not unreasonable to end it with another one.

> You are here to kneel
> Where prayer has been valid. And prayer is more
> Than an order of words, the conscious occupation
> Of the praying mind, or the sound of the voice praying.
> And what the dead had no speech for, when living,
> They can tell you, being dead: the communication
> Of the dead is tongued with fire beyond the language of the living.
> Here, the intersection of the timeless moment
> Is England and nowhere. Never and always.

———

O GOD, who has brought us near to an innumerable company of angels,
and to the spirits of just men made perfect;
grant us during our earthly pilgrimage to abide in their fellowship,
and in Your heavenly country to become partakers of their joy;
through Jesus Christ our Lord.
Amen.